A RAISIN IN THE SUN

Works by
LORRAINE HANSBERRY

A Raisin in the Sun

The Sign in Sidney Brustein's Window

The Drinking Gourd

To Be Young, Gifted and Black

Les Blancs

What Use Are Flowers?

The Movement

A
RAISIN
IN THE
SUN

LORRAINE HANSBERRY

With an Introduction by
Robert Nemiroff

VINTAGE BOOKS

A Division of Random House, Inc.

New York

FIRST VINTAGE BOOKS EDITION, DECEMBER 1994

Library of Congress Cataloging-in-Publication Data
Hansberry, Lorraine, 1930–1965.
A raisin in the sun / by Lorraine Hansberry; with an introduction
by Robert Nemiroff.—1st Vintage Books ed.
p.   cm.
ISBN 0-679-75533-0
1. Afro-Americans—History—20th century—Drama.   I. Title.
PS3515.A515R3   1994
812'.54—dc20   94-20636
CIP

Book design by Merrick Hamilton

Manufactured in the United States of America

68 67 66 65 64 63 62 61 60 59

To Mama:
in gratitude for the dream

What happens to a dream deferred?
Does it dry up
Like a raisin in the sun?
Or fester like a sore—
And then run?
Does it stink like rotten meat
Or crust and sugar over—
Like a syrupy sweet?

Maybe it just sags
Like a heavy load.

Or does it explode?

LANGSTON HUGHES

INTRODUCTION

by Robert Nemiroff

This is the most complete edition of *A Raisin in the Sun* ever published. Like the American Playhouse production for television, it restores to the play two scenes unknown to the general public, and a number of other key scenes and passages staged for the first time in twenty-fifth anniversary revivals and, most notably, the Roundabout Theatre's Kennedy Center production on which the television picture is based.

"The events of every passing year add resonance to *A Raisin in the Sun*. It is as if history is conspiring to make the play a classic"; ". . . one of a handful of great American dramas . . . *A Raisin in the Sun* belongs in the inner circle, along with *Death of a Salesman, Long Day's Journey into Night,* and *The Glass Menagerie.*" So wrote *The New York Times* and the *Washington Post* respectively of Harold Scott's revelatory stagings for the Roundabout in which most of these elements, cut on Broadway, were restored. The unprecedented resurgence of the work (a dozen regional revivals at this writing, new publications and productions abroad, and now the television production that will be seen by millions) prompts the new edition.

Produced in 1959, the play presaged the revolution in black and women's consciousness—and the revolutionary ferment in Africa—that exploded in the years following the playwright's death in 1965 to ineradicably alter the social fabric and consciousness of the nation and the world. As so many have commented lately, it did so in a manner and to an extent that few could have foreseen, for not only the restored material, but much else that passed unnoticed in

The late ROBERT NEMIROFF, Lorraine Hansberry's literary executor, shared a working relationship with the playwright from the time of their marriage in 1953. He was the producer and/or adapter of several of her works, including *The Sign in Sidney Brustein's Window; To Be Young, Gifted and Black;* and *Les Blancs.* In 1974, his production of the musical *Raisin,* based on *A Raisin in the Sun,* won the Tony Award for Best Musical.

the play at the time, speaks to issues that are now inescapable: value systems of the black family; concepts of African American beauty and identity; class and generational conflicts; the relationships of husbands and wives, black men and women; the outspoken (if then yet unnamed) feminism of the daughter; and, in the penultimate scene between Beneatha and Asagai, the larger statement of the play—and the ongoing struggle it portends.

Not one of the cuts, it should be emphasized, was made to dilute or censor the play or to "soften" its statement, for everyone in that herculean, now-legendary band that brought *Raisin* to Broadway—and most specifically the producer, Philip Rose, and director, Lloyd Richards—*believed* in the importance of that statement with a degree of commitment that would have countenanced nothing of the kind. How and why, then, did the cuts come about?

The scene in which Beneatha unveils her natural haircut is an interesting example. In 1959, when the play was presented, the rich variety of Afro styles introduced in the mid-sixties had not yet arrived: the very few black women who wore their hair unstraightened cut it very short. When the hair of Diana Sands (who created the role) was cropped in this fashion, however, a few days before the opening, it was not contoured to suit her: her particular facial structure required a fuller Afro, of the sort she in fact adopted in later years. Result? Rather than vitiate the playwright's point—the beauty of black hair—the scene was dropped.

Some cuts were similarly the result of happenstance or unpredictables of the kind that occur in any production: difficulties with a scene, the "processes" of actors, the dynamics of staging, etc. But most were related to the length of the play: running time. Time in the context of bringing to Broadway the first play by a black (young and unknown) woman, to be directed, moreover, by another unknown black "first," in a theater were black audiences virtually did not exist—and where, in the entire history of the American stage, there had never been a serious *commercially successful* black drama!

So unlikely did the prospects seem in that day, in fact,

to all but Phil Rose and the company, that much as some expressed admiration for the play, Rose's eighteen-month effort to find a co-producer to help complete the financing was turned down by virtually every established name in the business. He was joined at the last by another newcomer, David Cogan, but even with the money in hand, not a single theater owner on the Great White Way would *rent* to the new production! So that when the play left New York for tryouts—with a six-hundred-dollar advance in New Haven and no theater to come back to—had the script and performance been any less ready, and the response of critics and audiences any less unreserved than they proved to be, *A Raisin in the Sun* would never have reached Broadway.

Under these circumstances the pressures were enormous (if unspoken and rarely even acknowledged in the excitement of the work) *not* to press fate unduly with unnecessary risks. And the most obvious of these was the running time. It is one thing to present a four-and-a-half-hour drama by Eugene O'Neill on Broadway—but a *first* play (even ignoring the special features of this one) in the neighborhood of even *three*??? By common consensus, the need to keep the show as tight and streamlined as possible was manifest. Some things—philosophical flights, nuances the general audience might not understand, shadings, embellishments— would have to be sacrificed.

At the time the cuts were made (there were also some very good ones that focused and strengthened the drama), it was assumed by all that they would in no way significantly affect or alter the statement of the play, for there is nothing in the omitted lines that is not implicit elsewhere in, and throughout, *A Raisin in the Sun*. But to think this was to reckon without two factors the future would bring into play. The first was the swiftness and depth of the revolution in consciousness that was coming and the consequent, perhaps inevitable, tendency of some people to assume, because the "world" had changed, that *any* "successful" work which preceded the change must embody the values they had outgrown. And the second was the nature of the American audience.

James Baldwin has written that "Americans suffer from an ignorance that is not only colossal, but sacred." He is referring to that apparently endless capacity we have nurtured through long years to deceive ourselves where race is concerned: the baggage of myth and preconception we carry with us that enables northerners, for example, to shield themselves from the extent and virulence of segregation in the North, so that each time an "incident" of violence so egregious that they cannot look past it occurs they are "shocked" anew, as if it had never happened before or as if the problem were largely passé. (In 1975, when the cast of *Raisin*, the musical, became involved in defense of a family whose home in Queens, New York City, had been fire-bombed, we learned of a 1972 City Commissioner of Human Rights Report, citing "eleven cases *in the last eighteen months* in which minority-owned homes had been set afire or vandalized, a church had been bombed, and a school bus had been attacked"—in New York City!)

But Baldwin is referring also to the human capacity, where a work of art is involved, to substitute, for what the writer has written, what in our hearts we *wish* to believe. As Hansberry put it in response to one reviewer's enthusiastic if particularly misguided praise of her play: ". . . it did not disturb the writer in the least that there is no such implication in the entire three acts. He did not need it in the play; he had it in his head."[1]

Such problems did not, needless to say, stop America from embracing *A Raisin in the Sun*. But it did interfere drastically, for a generation, with the way the play was interpreted and assessed—and, in hindsight, it made all the more regrettable the abridgment (though without it would we even know the play today?). In a remarkable rumination on Hansberry's death, Ossie Davis (who succeeded Sidney Poitier in the role of Walter Lee) put it this way:

The play deserved all this—the playwright deserved all this, and more. Beyond question! But I have a feeling that for

[1]"Willie Loman, Walter Younger, and He Who Must Live," *Village Voice*, August 12, 1959.

all she got, Lorraine Hansberry never got all she deserved in regard to *A Raisin in the Sun*—that she got success, but that in her success she was cheated, both as a writer and as a Negro.

One of the biggest selling points about *Raisin*—filling the grapevine, riding the word-of-mouth, laying the foundation for its wide, wide acceptance—was how much the Younger family was just like any other American family. Some people were ecstatic to find that "it didn't really have to be about Negroes at all!" It was, rather, a walking, talking, living demonstration of our mythic conviction that, underneath, all of us Americans, *color-ain't-got-nothing-to-do-with-it*, are pretty much alike. People are just people, whoever they are; and all they want is a chance to be like other people. This uncritical assumption, sentimentally held by the audience, powerfully fixed in the character of the powerful mother with whom everybody could identify, immediately and completely, made any other questions about the Youngers, and what living in the slums of Southside Chicago had done to them, not only irrelevant and impertinent, but also disloyal . . . because everybody who walked into the theater saw in Lena Younger . . . his own great American Mama. And that was decisive.[1]

In effect, as Davis went on to develop, white America "kidnapped" Mama, stole her away and used her fantasized image to avoid what was uniquely *African* American in the play. And what it was saying.

Thus, in many reviews (and later academic studies), the Younger family—maintained by two female domestics and a chauffeur, son of a laborer dead of a lifetime of hard labor—was transformed into an acceptably "middle class" family. The decision to move became a desire to "integrate" (rather than, as Mama says simply, "to find the nicest house for the least amount of money for my family. . . . Them houses they put up for colored in them areas way out always seem to cost twice as much.").

[1]"The Significance of Lorraine Hansberry," *Freedomways*, Summer 1985.

In his "A Critical Reevaluation: *A Raisin in the Sun*'s Enduring Passion," Amiri Baraka comments aptly: "We missed the essence of the work—that Hansberry had created a family on the cutting edge of the same class and ideological struggles as existed in the movement itself and among the people. . . . The Younger family is part of the black majority, and the concerns I once dismissed as 'middle class'—buying a home and moving into 'white folks' neighborhoods'—are actually reflective of the essence of black people's striving and the will to defeat segregation, discrimination, and national oppression. There is no such thing as a 'white folks' neighborhood' except to racists *and to those submitting to racism*."[1]

Mama herself—about whose "acceptance" of her "place" in the society there is not a word in the play, and who, in quest of her family's survival over the soul- and body-crushing conditions of the ghetto, is prepared to defy housing-pattern taboos, threats, bombs, and God knows what else—became the safely "conservative" matriarch, upholder of the social order and proof that if one only perseveres with faith, everything will come out right in the end and the-system-ain't-so-bad-after-all. (All this, presumably, because, true to character, she speaks and thinks in the *language* of her generation, shares their dream of a better life and, like millions of her counterparts, takes her Christianity to heart.) At the same time, necessarily, Big Walter Younger—the husband who reared this family with her and whose unseen presence and influence can be heard in every scene—vanished from analysis.

And perhaps most ironical of all to the playwright, who had herself as a child been almost killed in such a real-life story,[2] the climax of the play became, pure and simple, a "happy ending"—despite the fact that it leaves the Youngers on the brink of what will surely be, in their new home,

---

[1]*A Raisin in the Sun and The Sign in Sidney Brustein's Window*, Vintage Books, 1995.
[2]Hansberry, *To Be Young, Gifted and Black*, New American Library, p. 51.

at *best* a nightmare of uncertainty. ("If he thinks that's a happy ending," said Hansberry in an interview, "I invite him to come live in one of the communities where the Youngers are going!"[1]) Which is not even to mention the fact that that little house in a blue-collar neighborhood— hardly suburbia, as some have imagined—is hardly the answer to the deeper needs and inequities of race and class and sex that Walter and Beneatha have articulated.

When Lorraine Hansberry read the reviews—delighted by the accolades, grateful for the recognition, but also deeply troubled—she decided in short order to put back many of the materials excised. She did that in the 1959 Random House edition, but faced with the actuality of a prize-winning play, she hesitated about some others which, for reasons now beside the point, had not in rehearsal come alive. She later felt, however, that the full last scene between Beneatha and Asagai (drastically cut on Broadway) and Walter's bedtime scene with Travis (eliminated entirely) should be restored at the first opportunity, and this was done in the 1966 New American Library edition. As anyone who has seen the recent productions will attest, they are among the most moving (and most applauded) moments in the play.

Because the visit of Mrs. Johnson adds the costs of another character to the cast and ten more minutes to the play, it has not been used in most revivals. But where it has been tried it has worked to solid—often hilarious—effect. It can be seen in the American Playhouse production, and is included here in any case, because it speaks to fundamental issues of the play, makes plain the reality that waits the Youngers at the curtain, and, above all, makes clear what, in the eyes of the author, Lena Younger—in her typicality within the black experience—does and does *not* represent.

Another scene—the Act I, Scene Two moment in which Beneatha observes and Travis gleefully recounts his latest

---

[1]"Make New Sounds: Studs Terkel Interviews Lorraine Hansberry," *American Theatre*, November 1984.

adventure in the street below—makes tangible and visceral one of the many facts of ghetto life that impel the Youngers' move. As captured on television and published here for the first time, it is its own sobering comment on just how "middle class" a family this is.

A word about the stage and interpretive directions. These are the author's original directions combined, where meaningful to the reader,[1] with the staging insights of two great directors and companies: Lloyd Richards' classic staging of that now-legendary cast that first created the roles; and Harold Scott's, whose searching explorations of the text in successive revivals over many years—culminating in the inspired production that broke box office records at the Kennedy Center and won ten awards for Scott and the company—have given the fuller text, in my view, its most definitive realization to date.

Finally, a note about the American Playhouse production. Unlike the drastically cut and largely one-dimensional 1961 movie version—which, affecting and pioneering though it may have been, reflected little of the greatness of the original stage performances—this new screen version is a luminous embodiment of the stage play as reconceived, but not altered, for the camera, and is exquisitely performed. That it is, is due inextricably to producer Chiz Schultz's and director Bill Duke's unswerving commitment to the text; Harold Scott's formative work with the stage company; Duke's own fresh insights and the cinematic brilliance of his reconception and direction for the screen; and the energizing infusion into this mix of Danny Glover's classic performance as Walter Lee to Esther Rolle's superlative Mama. As in the case of any production, I am apt to question a nuance here and there, and regrettably, because of a happenstance in production, the Walter-Travis scene has been omitted. But that scene will, I expect, be restored in the videocassette version of the picture, which should be available shortly. It is thus an excellent version for study.

[1] Much fuller directions for staging purposes are contained in the Samuel French Thirtieth Anniversary acting edition.

What is for me personally, as a witness to and sometime participant in the foregoing events, most gratifying about the current revival is that today, some twenty-nine years after Lorraine Hansberry, thinking back with disbelief a few nights after the opening of *Raisin*, typed out these words—

> . . . I had turned the last page out of the typewriter and pressed all the sheets neatly together in a pile, and gone and stretched out face down on the living room floor. I had finished a play; a play I had no reason to think or not think would ever be done; a play that I was sure no one would quite understand. . . .[1]

—her play is not only being done, but that more than she had ever thought possible—and more clearly than it ever has been before—it is being "understood."

Yet one last point that I must make because it has come up so many times of late. I have been asked if I am not surprised that the play still remains so contemporary, and isn't that a "sad" commentary on America? It is indeed a sad commentary, but the question also assumed something more: that it is the topicality of the play's immediate events—i.e., the persistence of white opposition to unrestricted housing and the ugly manifestations of racism in its myriad forms—that keeps it alive. But I don't believe that such alone is what explains its vitality at all. For though the specifics of social mores and societal patterns will always change, the decline of the "New England territory" and the institution of the traveling salesman does not, for example, "date" *Death of a Salesman*, any more than the fact that we now recognize *love* (as opposed to interfamilial politics) as a legitimate basis for marriage obviates *Romeo and Juliet*. If we ever reach a time when the racial madness that afflicts America is at last truly behind us—as obviously *we must* if we are to survive in a world composed four-fifths of peoples of color—then I believe *A Raisin in the Sun* will remain no less pertinent. For at the deepest level it is not

[1] *To Be Young, Gifted and Black*, p. 120.

a specific situation but the human condition, human aspiration, and human relationships—the persistence of dreams, of the bonds and conflicts between men and women, parents and children, old ways and new, and the endless struggle against human oppression, whatever the forms it may take, and for individual fulfillment, recognition, and liberation—that are at the heart of such plays. It is not surprising therefore that in each generation we recognize ourselves in them anew.

Croton-on-Hudson, N.Y.
October 1988

ACKNOWLEDGMENTS

In addition to individuals and institutions recalled above and in the American Playhouse and Broadway credits—and the many others too numerous to record who have contributed to the current revival—I wish especially to thank:

- Gene Feist and Todd Haimes of the Roundabout Theatre, without whom what followed could never have been;
- Burt D'Lugoff, Howard Hausman, Alan Bomser, and Seymour Baldash, whose support and critical judgment have been invaluable;
- Jaki Brown, Toni Livingston, and Josephine Abady, who first dared to dream and then to break the first ground to bring *Raisin* to television;
- Esther Rolle and all in the Roundabout *Raisin* "family" whose unwavering commitment through three on-again, off-again, touch-and-go years were the rock on which the production stood;
- Danny Glover, whose name, alongside Ms. Rolle's, made the production possible but did not prepare one for the magnificent actuality of his work;
- David M. Davis and Lindsay Law of American Playhouse; Ricki Franklin, Phylis Geller, and Samuel J. Paul of KCET/Los Angeles; and David Loxton and WNET/New York—who extended every cooperation and maximum freedom for us to develop and produce the television production as we saw it; and
- Producer Chiz Schultz and co-producer Steve Schwartz, who brought to the new incarnation not only impeccable judgment and assured expertise, but an integrity of caring dedication to the playwright's vision and text that one meets rarely, if ever, at the crossroads of art and commerce.

I regret that there is not the space to name here, too, each of the wonderful actors, understudies, designers, technicians, and staff of both the Roundabout and television productions who do not appear in the Playhouse credits, but whose contributions and spirits are joined to those of their colleagues on screen. I am indebted to them all.

And, finally, two in a place by themselves:

- My wife, Jewell Handy Gresham, who has stood unbending through the worst and the best of times, providing light and unfailing inspiration to the vision we share; and

- Samuel Liff of the William Morris Agency, without whose personal commitment and extraordinary perseverance going far beyond the professional to a true love of theater and art, *much* that has happened could never have been.

R.N.

1988

A RAISIN IN THE SUN

The American Playhouse television presentation of A RAISIN IN THE SUN, *broadcast on February 1, 1989, was a production of* Robert Nemiroff/Jaki Brown/Toni Livingston/Josephine Abady Productions, Fireside Entertainment Corporation, *and* KCET/Los Angeles *in association with* WNET/New York.

CAST

(in order of appearance)

RUTH YOUNGER	Starletta DuPois
WALTER LEE YOUNGER	Danny Glover
TRAVIS YOUNGER	Kimble Joyner
BENEATHA YOUNGER	Kim Yancey
LENA YOUNGER	Esther Rolle
JOSEPH ASAGAI	Lou Ferguson
GEORGE MURCHISON	Joseph C. Phillips
MRS. JOHNSON	Helen Martin
KARL LINDNER	John Fiedler
BOBO	Stephen Henderson
MOVING MEN	Ron O.J. Parson, Charles Watts

Directed by Bill Duke
Produced by Chiz Schultz
Executive Producer Robert Nemiroff

Co-Producer	*Production Design*
Steven S. Schwartz	Thomas Cariello

Lighting Design	*Costume Design*
Bill Klages	Celia Bryant *and* Judy Dearing

Music	*Edited by*
Ed Bland	Gary Anderson

Camerawork
Greg Cook, Gregory Harms, Kenneth A. Patterson

*(Based on the 25th Anniversary Stage Production
Directed by* Harold Scott
Produced by The Roundabout Theatre Company, Inc.
[Gene Feist/Todd Haimes] *and* Robert Nemiroff)

Produced for American Playhouse with funds from Public Television Stations, the Corporation for Public Broadcasting, the National Endowment for the Arts, and the Chubb Group of Insurance Companies. American Playhouse is presented by KCET, SCETV, WGBH, *and* WNET; *Executive Director* David M. Davis, *Executive Producer* Lindsay Law, *Director of Program Development* Lynn Holst. *For* KCET: *Executive Producer* Ricki Franklin, *Supervising Producer* Samuel J. Paul, *Executive in Charge* Phylis Geller; *with additional funds from the Ambassador International Foundation. For* WNET: *Executive Producer* David Loxton.

A RAISIN IN THE SUN *was first presented by Philip Rose and David J. Cogan at the Ethel Barrymore Theatre, New York City, March 11, 1959, with the following cast:*

(In order of appearance)

RUTH YOUNGER	Ruby Dee
TRAVIS YOUNGER	Glynn Turman
WALTER LEE YOUNGER (BROTHER)	Sidney Poitier
BENEATHA YOUNGER	Diana Sands
LENA YOUNGER (MAMA)	Claudia McNeil
JOSEPH ASAGAI	Ivan Dixon
GEORGE MURCHISON	Louis Gossett
KARL LINDNER	John Fiedler
BOBO	Lonne Elder III
MOVING MEN	Ed Hall, Douglas Turner Ward

Directed by Lloyd Richards

Designed and Lighted by Ralph Alswang

Costumes by Virginia Volland

The action of the play is set
in Chicago's Southside, sometime between
World War II and the present.

Act I
Scene One: Friday morning.
Scene Two: The following morning.

Act II
Scene One: Later, the same day.
Scene Two: Friday night, a few weeks later.
Scene Three: Moving day, one week later.

Act III
An hour later.

ACT I

SCENE ONE

The YOUNGER *living room would be a comfortable and well-ordered room if it were not for a number of indestructible contradictions to this state of being. Its furnishings are typical and undistinguished and their primary feature now is that they have clearly had to accommodate the living of too many people for too many years—and they are tired. Still, we can see that at some time, a time probably no longer remembered by the family (except perhaps for* MAMA), *the furnishings of this room were actually selected with care and love and even hope—and brought to this apartment and arranged with taste and pride.*

That was a long time ago. Now the once loved pattern of the couch upholstery has to fight to show itself from under acres of crocheted doilies and couch covers which have themselves finally come to be more important than the upholstery. And here a table or a chair has been moved to disguise the worn places in the carpet; but the carpet has fought back by showing its weariness, with depressing uniformity, elsewhere on its surface.

Weariness has, in fact, won in this room. Everything has been polished, washed, sat on, used, scrubbed too often. All pretenses but living itself have long since vanished from the very atmosphere of this room.

Moreover, a section of this room, for it is not really a room unto itself, though the landlord's lease would make it seem so, slopes backward to provide a small kitchen area, where the family prepares the meals that are eaten in the living room proper, which must also serve as dining room. The single window that has been provided for these "two" rooms is located in this kitchen area. The sole natural light the family may enjoy in the course of a day is only that which fights its way through this little window.

At left, a door leads to a bedroom which is shared by MAMA *and her daughter,* BENEATHA. *At right, opposite, is a second room (which in the beginning of the life of this apartment was probably a breakfast room) which serves as a bedroom for* WALTER *and his wife,* RUTH.

Time: Sometime between World War II and the present.
Place: Chicago's Southside.

At Rise: It is morning dark in the living room. TRAVIS *is asleep on the make-down bed at center. An alarm clock sounds from within the bedroom at right, and presently* RUTH *enters from that room and closes the door behind her. She crosses sleepily toward the window. As she passes her sleeping son she reaches down and shakes him a little. At the window she raises the shade and a dusky Southside morning light comes in feebly. She fills a pot with water and puts it on to boil. She calls to the boy, between yawns, in a slightly muffled voice.*

RUTH *is about thirty. We can see that she was a pretty girl, even exceptionally so, but now it is apparent that life has been little that she expected, and disappointment has already begun to hang in her face. In a few years, before thirty-five even, she will be known among her people as a "settled woman."*

She crosses to her son and gives him a good, final, rousing shake.

RUTH Come on now, boy, it's seven thirty! *(Her son sits up at last, in a stupor of sleepiness)* I say hurry up, Travis! You ain't the only person in the world got to use a bathroom! *(The child, a sturdy, handsome little boy of ten or eleven, drags himself out of the bed and almost blindly takes his towels and "today's clothes" from drawers and a closet and goes out to the bathroom, which is in an outside hall and which is shared by another family or families on the same floor. RUTH crosses to the bedroom door at right and opens it and calls in to her husband)* Walter Lee! . . . It's after seven thirty! Lemme see you do some waking up in there now! *(She waits)* You better get up from there, man! It's after seven thirty I tell you. *(She waits again)* All right, you just go ahead and lay there and next thing you know Travis be finished and Mr. Johnson'll be in there and you'll be fussing and cussing round here like a madman! And be late too! *(She waits, at the end of patience)* Walter Lee—it's time for you to GET UP!

(She waits another second and then starts to go into the bedroom, but is apparently satisfied that her husband has begun to get up. She stops, pulls the door to, and returns to the kitchen area. She wipes her face with a moist cloth and runs her fingers through her sleep-disheveled hair in a vain effort and ties an apron around her housecoat. The bedroom door at right opens and her husband stands in the doorway in his pajamas, which are rumpled and mismated. He is a lean, intense young man in his middle thirties, inclined to quick nervous movements and erratic speech habits—and always in his voice there is a quality of indictment)

WALTER Is he out yet?

RUTH What you mean *out*? He ain't hardly got in there good yet.

WALTER *(Wandering in, still more oriented to sleep than to a new day)* Well, what was you doing all that yelling for if I can't even get in there yet? *(Stopping and thinking)* Check coming today?

RUTH They *said* Saturday and this is just Friday and I hopes to God you ain't going to get up here first thing this morning and start talking to me 'bout no money— 'cause I 'bout don't want to hear it.

WALTER Something the matter with you this morning?

RUTH No—I'm just sleepy as the devil. What kind of eggs you want?

WALTER Not scrambled. (RUTH *starts to scramble eggs)* Paper come? (RUTH *points impatiently to the rolled up* Tribune *on the table, and he gets it and spreads it out and vaguely reads the front page)* Set off another bomb yesterday.

RUTH *(Maximum indifference)* Did they?

WALTER *(Looking up)* What's the matter with you?

RUTH Ain't nothing the matter with me. And don't keep asking me that this morning.

WALTER Ain't nobody bothering you. *(Reading the news of the day absently again)* Say Colonel McCormick is sick.

RUTH *(Affecting tea-party interest)* Is he now? Poor thing.

WALTER *(Sighing and looking at his watch)* Oh, me. *(He waits)* Now what is that boy doing in that bathroom all this time? He just going to have to start getting up earlier. I can't be being late to work on account of him fooling around in there.

RUTH *(Turning on him)* Oh, no he ain't going to be getting up no earlier no such thing! It ain't his fault that he can't get to bed no earlier nights 'cause he got a bunch of crazy good-for-nothing clowns sitting up running their mouths in what is supposed to be his bedroom after ten o'clock at night . . .

WALTER That's what you mad about, ain't it? The things I want to talk about with my friends just couldn't be important in your mind, could they?
(He rises and finds a cigarette in her handbag on the table and crosses to the little window and looks out, smoking and deeply enjoying this first one)

RUTH *(Almost matter of factly, a complaint too automatic to deserve emphasis)* Why you always got to smoke before you eat in the morning?

WALTER *(At the window)* Just look at 'em down there . . . Running and racing to work . . . *(He turns and faces his wife and watches her a moment at the stove, and then, suddenly)* You look young this morning, baby.

RUTH *(Indifferently)* Yeah?

WALTER Just for a second—stirring them eggs. Just for a second it was—you looked real young again. *(He reaches for her; she crosses away. Then, drily)* It's gone now—you look like yourself again!

RUTH Man, if you don't shut up and leave me alone.

WALTER *(Looking out to the street again)* First thing a man ought to learn in life is not to make love to no colored woman first thing in the morning. You all some eeeevil people at eight o'clock in the morning.
(TRAVIS appears in the hall doorway, almost fully dressed and quite wide awake now, his towels and pajamas across his shoulders. He opens the door and signals for his father to make the bathroom in a hurry)

TRAVIS *(Watching the bathroom)* Daddy, come on!
(WALTER gets his bathroom utensils and flies out to the bathroom)

RUTH Sit down and have your breakfast, Travis.

TRAVIS Mama, this is Friday. *(Gleefully)* Check coming tomorrow, huh?

RUTH You get your mind off money and eat your breakfast.

TRAVIS *(Eating)* This is the morning we supposed to bring the fifty cents to school.

RUTH Well, I ain't got no fifty cents this morning.

TRAVIS Teacher say we have to.

RUTH I don't care what teacher say. I ain't got it. Eat your breakfast, Travis.

TRAVIS I *am* eating.

RUTH Hush up now and just eat!
(The boy gives her an exasperated look for her lack of understanding, and eats grudgingly)

TRAVIS You think Grandmama would have it?

RUTH No! And I want you to stop asking your grandmother for money, you hear me?

TRAVIS *(Outraged)* Gaaaleee! I don't ask her, she just gimme it sometimes!

RUTH Travis Willard Younger—I got too much on me this morning to be—

TRAVIS Maybe Daddy—

RUTH *Travis!*
(The boy hushes abruptly. They are both quiet and tense for several seconds)

TRAVIS *(Presently)* Could I maybe go carry some groceries in front of the supermarket for a little while after school then?

RUTH Just hush, I said. *(Travis jabs his spoon into his cereal bowl viciously, and rests his head in anger upon his fists)* If you through eating, you can get over there and make up your bed.
(The boy obeys stiffly and crosses the room, almost mechanically, to the bed and more or less folds the bedding into a heap, then angrily gets his books and cap)

TRAVIS *(Sulking and standing apart from her unnaturally)* I'm gone.

RUTH *(Looking up from the stove to inspect him automatically)* Come here. *(He crosses to her and she studies his head)* If you don't take this comb and fix this here head, you better! *(TRAVIS puts down his books with a great sigh of oppression, and crosses to the mirror. His mother mutters under her breath about his "slubbornness")* 'Bout to march out of here with that head looking just like chickens slept in it! I just don't know where you get your slubborn ways . . . And get your jacket, too. Looks chilly out this morning.

TRAVIS *(With conspicuously brushed hair and jacket)* I'm gone.

RUTH Get carfare and milk money—*(Waving one finger)*—and not a single penny for no caps, you hear me?

TRAVIS *(With sullen politeness)* Yes'm.
(He turns in outrage to leave. His mother watches after him as in his frustration he approaches the door almost comically. When she speaks to him, her voice has become a very gentle tease)

RUTH *(Mocking; as she thinks he would say it)* Oh, Mama makes me so mad sometimes, I don't know what to do! *(She waits and continues to his back as he stands stock-still in front of the door)* I wouldn't kiss that woman good-bye for nothing in this world this morning! *(The boy finally turns around and rolls his eyes at her, knowing the mood has changed and he is vindicated; he does not, however, move toward her yet)* Not for nothing in this world! *(She finally laughs aloud at him and holds out her arms to him and we see that it is a way between them, very old and practiced. He crosses to her and allows her to embrace him warmly but keeps his face fixed with masculine rigidity. She holds him back from her presently and looks at him and runs her fingers over the features of his face. With utter gentleness—)* Now—whose little old angry man are you?

TRAVIS *(The masculinity and gruffness start to fade at last)* Aw gaalee—Mama . . .

RUTH *(Mimicking)* Aw gaaaaalleeeee, Mama! *(She pushes him, with rough playfulness and finality, toward the door)* Get on out of here or you going to be late.

TRAVIS *(In the face of love, new aggressiveness)* Mama, could I *please* go carry groceries?

RUTH Honey, it's starting to get so cold evenings.

WALTER *(Coming in from the bathroom and drawing a make-believe gun from a make-believe holster and shooting at his son)* What is it he wants to do?

RUTH Go carry groceries after school at the supermarket.

WALTER Well, let him go . . .

TRAVIS *(Quickly, to the ally)* I *have* to—she won't gimme the fifty cents . . .

WALTER *(To his wife only)* Why not?

RUTH *(Simply, and with flavor)* 'Cause we don't have it.

WALTER *(To* RUTH *only)* What you tell the boy things like that for? *(Reaching down into his pants with a rather important gesture)* Here, son—
(He hands the boy the coin, but his eyes are directed to his wife's. TRAVIS *takes the money happily)*

TRAVIS Thanks, Daddy.
(He starts out. RUTH *watches both of them with murder in her eyes.* WALTER *stands and stares back at her with defiance, and suddenly reaches into his pocket again on an afterthought)*

WALTER *(Without even looking at his son, still staring hard at his wife)* In fact, here's another fifty cents . . . Buy yourself some fruit today—or take a taxicab to school or something!

TRAVIS Whoopee—
(He leaps up and clasps his father around the middle with his legs, and they face each other in mutual appreciation; slowly WALTER LEE *peeks around the boy to catch the violent rays from his wife's eyes and draws his head back as if shot)*

WALTER You better get down now—and get to school, man.

TRAVIS *(At the door)* O.K. Good-bye.
(He exits)

WALTER *(After him, pointing with pride)* That's *my* boy.
(She looks at him in disgust and turns back to her work)
You know what I was thinking 'bout in the bathroom this morning?

RUTH No.

WALTER How come you always try to be so pleasant!

RUTH What is there to be pleasant 'bout!

WALTER You want to know what I was thinking 'bout in the bathroom or not!

RUTH I know what you thinking 'bout.

WALTER (*Ignoring her*) 'Bout what me and Willy Harris was talking about last night.

RUTH (*Immediately—a refrain*) Willy Harris is a good-for-nothing loudmouth.

WALTER Anybody who talks to me has got to be a good-for-nothing loudmouth, ain't he? And what you know about who is just a good-for-nothing loudmouth? Charlie Atkins was just a "good-for-nothing loudmouth" too, wasn't he! When he wanted me to go in the dry-cleaning business with him. And now—he's grossing a hundred thousand a year. A hundred thousand dollars a year! You still call *him* a loudmouth!

RUTH (*Bitterly*) Oh, Walter Lee . . .
   (*She folds her head on her arms over the table*)

WALTER (*Rising and coming to her and standing over her*) You tired, ain't you? Tired of everything. Me, the boy, the way we live—this beat-up hole—everything. Ain't you? (*She doesn't look up, doesn't answer*) So tired—moaning and groaning all the time, but you wouldn't do nothing to help, would you? You couldn't be on my side that long for nothing, could you?

RUTH Walter, please leave me alone.

WALTER A man needs for a woman to back him up . . .

RUTH Walter—

WALTER Mama would listen to you. You know she listen to you more than she do me and Bennie. She think more of you. All you have to do is just sit down with her when you drinking your coffee one morning and talking 'bout things like you do and—(*He sits down be-*

side her and demonstrates graphically what he thinks her methods and tone should be)—you just sip your coffee, see, and say easy like that you been thinking 'bout that deal Walter Lee is so interested in, 'bout the store and all, and sip some more coffee, like what you saying ain't really that important to you— And the next thing you know, she be listening good and asking you questions and when I come home—I can tell her the details. This ain't no fly-by-night proposition, baby. I mean we figured it out, me and Willy and Bobo.

RUTH *(With a frown)* Bobo?

WALTER Yeah. You see, this little liquor store we got in mind cost seventy-five thousand and we figured the initial investment on the place be 'bout thirty thousand, see. That be ten thousand each. Course, there's a couple of hundred you got to pay so's you don't spend your life just waiting for them clowns to let your license get approved—

RUTH You mean graft?

WALTER *(Frowning impatiently)* Don't call it that. See there, that just goes to show you what women understand about the world. Baby, don't *nothing* happen for you in this world 'less you pay *somebody* off!

RUTH Walter, leave me alone! *(She raises her head and stares at him vigorously—then says, more quietly)* Eat your eggs, they gonna be cold.

WALTER *(Straightening up from her and looking off)* That's it. There you are. Man say to his woman: I got me a dream. His woman say: Eat your eggs. *(Sadly, but gaining in power)* Man say: I got to take hold of this here world, baby! And a woman will say: Eat your eggs and go to work. *(Passionately now)* Man say: I got to change my life, I'm choking to death, baby! And his woman say—*(In utter anguish as he brings his fists down on his thighs)*—Your eggs is getting cold!

RUTH *(Softly)* Walter, that ain't none of our money.

WALTER *(Not listening at all or even looking at her)* This morning, I was lookin' in the mirror and thinking about it . . . I'm thirty-five years old; I been married eleven years and I got a boy who sleeps in the living room—*(Very, very quietly)*—and all I got to give him is stories about how rich white people live . . .

RUTH Eat your eggs, Walter.

WALTER *(Slams the table and jumps up)*—DAMN MY EGGS—DAMN ALL THE EGGS THAT EVER WAS!

RUTH Then go to work.

WALTER *(Looking up at her)* See—I'm trying to talk to you 'bout myself—*(Shaking his head with the repetition)*—and all you can say is eat them eggs and go to work.

RUTH *(Wearily)* Honey, you never say nothing new. I listen to you every day, every night and every morning, and you never say nothing new. *(Shrugging)* So you would rather *be* Mr. Arnold than be his chauffeur. So—I would *rather* be living in Buckingham Palace.

WALTER That is just what is wrong with the colored woman in this world . . . Don't understand about building their men up and making 'em feel like they somebody. Like they can do something.

RUTH *(Drily, but to hurt)* There are colored men who do things.

WALTER No thanks to the colored woman.

RUTH Well, being a colored woman, I guess I can't help myself none.
      (She rises and gets the ironing board and sets it

up and attacks a huge pile of rough-dried clothes, sprin-
kling them in preparation for the ironing and then
rolling them into tight fat balls)

WALTER *(Mumbling)* We one group of men tied to a race
of women with small minds!

> *(His sister* BENEATHA *enters. She is about twenty, as*
> *slim and intense as her brother. She is not as pretty*
> *as her sister-in-law, but her lean, almost intellec-*
> *tual face has a handsomeness of its own. She wears a*
> *bright-red flannel nightie, and her thick hair stands*
> *wildly about her head. Her speech is a mixture of*
> *many things; it is different from the rest of the fam-*
> *ily's insofar as education has permeated her sense*
> *of English—and perhaps the Midwest rather than*
> *the South has finally—at last—won out in her in-*
> *flection; but not altogether, because over all of it is*
> *a soft slurring and transformed use of vowels which*
> *is the decided influence of the Southside. She passes*
> *through the room without looking at either* RUTH
> *or* WALTER *and goes to the outside door and looks,*
> *a little blindly, out to the bathroom. She sees that*
> *it has been lost to the Johnsons. She closes the door*
> *with a sleepy vengeance and crosses to the table and*
> *sits down a little defeated)*

BENEATHA I am going to start timing those people.

WALTER You should get up earlier.

BENEATHA *(Her face in her hands. She is still fighting the*
urge to go back to bed) Really—would you suggest
dawn? Where's the paper?

WALTER *(Pushing the paper across the table to her as he*
studies her almost clinically, as though he has never
seen her before) You a horrible-looking chick at this
hour.

BENEATHA *(Drily)* Good morning, everybody.

WALTER *(Senselessly)* How is school coming?

BENEATHA *(In the same spirit)* Lovely. Lovely. And you know, biology is the greatest. *(Looking up at him)* I dissected something that looked just like you yesterday.

WALTER I just wondered if you've made up your mind and everything.

BENEATHA *(Gaining in sharpness and impatience)* And what did I answer yesterday morning—and the day before that?

RUTH *(From the ironing board, like someone disinterested and old)* Don't be so nasty, Bennie.

BENEATHA *(Still to her brother)* And the day before that and the day before that!

WALTER *(Defensively)* I'm interested in you. Something wrong with that? Ain't many girls who decide—

WALTER *and* BENEATHA *(In unison)* —"to be a doctor." *(Silence)*

WALTER Have we figured out yet just exactly how much medical school is going to cost?

RUTH Walter Lee, why don't you leave that girl alone and get out of here to work?

BENEATHA *(Exits to the bathroom and bangs on the door)* Come on out of there, please!
(She comes back into the room)

WALTER *(Looking at his sister intently)* You know the check is coming tomorrow.

BENEATHA *(Turning on him with a sharpness all her own)* That money belongs to Mama, Walter, and it's for her to decide how she wants to use it. I don't care if she wants to buy a house or a rocket ship or just nail it up somewhere and look at it. It's hers. Not ours—*hers*.

WALTER *(Bitterly)* Now ain't that fine! You just got your mother's interest at heart, ain't you, girl? You such a nice girl—but if Mama got that money she can always take a few thousand and help you through school too—can't she?

BENEATHA I have never asked anyone around here to do anything for me!

WALTER No! And the line between asking and just accepting when the time comes is big and wide—ain't it!

BENEATHA *(With fury)* What do you want from me, Brother—that I quit school or just drop dead, which!

WALTER I don't want nothing but for you to stop acting holy 'round here. Me and Ruth done made some sacrifices for you—why can't you do something for the family?

RUTH Walter, don't be dragging me in it.

WALTER You are in it— Don't you get up and go work in somebody's kitchen for the last three years to help put clothes on her back?

RUTH Oh, Walter—that's not fair . . .

WALTER It ain't that nobody expects you to get on your knees and say thank you, Brother; thank you, Ruth; thank you, Mama—and thank you, Travis, for wearing the same pair of shoes for two semesters—

BENEATHA *(Dropping to her knees)* Well—I *do*—all right?—thank everybody! And forgive me for ever wanting to be anything at all! *(Pursuing him on her knees across the floor)* FORGIVE ME, FORGIVE ME, FORGIVE ME!

RUTH Please stop it! Your mama'll hear you.

WALTER Who the hell told you you had to be a doctor?
If you so crazy 'bout messing 'round with sick people—
then go be a nurse like other women—or just get married
and be quiet . . .

BENEATHA Well—you finally got it said . . . It took you
three years but you finally got it said. Walter, give up;
leave me alone—it's Mama's money.

WALTER *He was my father, too!*

BENEATHA So what? He was mine, too—and Travis' grandfather—but the insurance money belongs to Mama. Picking on me is not going to make her give it to you to
invest in any liquor stores—*(Underbreath, dropping into
a chair)*—and I for one say, God bless Mama for that!

WALTER *(To* RUTH*)* See—did you hear? Did you hear!

RUTH Honey, please go to work.

WALTER Nobody in this house is ever going to understand
me.

BENEATHA Because you're a nut.

WALTER Who's a nut?

BENEATHA You—you are a nut. Thee is mad, boy.

WALTER *(Looking at his wife and his sister from the door,
very sadly)* The world's most backward race of people,
and that's a fact.

BENEATHA *(Turning slowly in her chair)* And then there
are all those prophets who would lead us out of the
wilderness—*(WALTER slams out of the house)*—into the
swamps!

RUTH Bennie, why you always gotta be pickin' on your

brother? Can't you be a little sweeter sometimes? *(Door opens.* WALTER *walks in. He fumbles with his cap, starts to speak, clears throat, looks everywhere but at* RUTH. *Finally:)*

WALTER *(To* RUTH*)* I need some money for carfare.

RUTH *(Looks at him, then warms; teasing, but tenderly)* Fifty cents? *(She goes to her bag and gets money)* Here—take a taxi!

*(*WALTER *exits.* MAMA *enters. She is a woman in her early sixties, full-bodied and strong. She is one of those women of a certain grace and beauty who wear it so unobtrusively that it takes a while to notice. Her dark-brown face is surrounded by the total whiteness of her hair, and, being a woman who has adjusted to many things in life and overcome many more, her face is full of strength. She has, we can see, wit and faith of a kind that keep her eyes lit and full of interest and expectancy. She is, in a word, a beautiful woman. Her bearing is perhaps most like the noble bearing of the women of the Hereros of Southwest Africa—rather as if she imagines that as she walks she still bears a basket or a vessel upon her head. Her speech, on the other hand, is as careless as her carriage is precise—she is inclined to slur everything— but her voice is perhaps not so much quiet as simply soft)*

MAMA Who that 'round here slamming doors at this hour?
(She crosses through the room, goes to the window, opens it, and brings in a feeble little plant growing doggedly in a small pot on the windowsill. She feels the dirt and puts it back out)

RUTH That was Walter Lee. He and Bennie was at it again.

MAMA My children and they tempers. Lord, if this little old plant don't get more sun than it's been getting it ain't never going to see spring again. *(She turns from the window)* What's the matter with you this morning, Ruth? You looks right peaked. You aiming to iron all them things? Leave some for me. I'll get to 'em this afternoon. Bennie honey, it's too drafty for you to be sitting 'round half dressed. Where's your robe?

BENEATHA In the cleaners.

MAMA Well, go get mine and put it on.

BENEATHA I'm not cold, Mama, honest.

MAMA I know—but you so thin . . .

BENEATHA *(Irritably)* Mama, I'm not cold.

MAMA *(Seeing the make-down bed as* TRAVIS *has left it)* Lord have mercy, look at that poor bed. Bless his heart— he tries, don't he?
(She moves to the bed TRAVIS *has sloppily made up)*

RUTH No—he don't half try at all 'cause he knows you going to come along behind him and fix everything. That's just how come he don't know how to do nothing right now—you done spoiled that boy so.

MAMA *(Folding bedding)* Well—he's a little boy. Ain't supposed to know 'bout housekeeping. My baby, that's what he is. What you fix for his breakfast this morning?

RUTH *(Angrily)* I feed my son, Lena!

MAMA I ain't meddling—*(Underbreath; busy-bodyish)* I just noticed all last week he had cold cereal, and when it starts getting this chilly in the fall a child ought to have some hot grits or something when he goes out in the cold—

RUTH *(Furious)* I gave him hot oats—is that all right!

MAMA I ain't meddling. *(Pause)* Put a lot of nice butter on it? *(RUTH shoots her an angry look and does not reply)* He likes lots of butter.

RUTH *(Exasperated)* Lena—

MAMA *(To BENEATHA. MAMA is inclined to wander conversationally sometimes)* What was you and your brother fussing 'bout this morning?

BENEATHA It's not important, Mama.
   (She gets up and goes to look out at the bathroom, which is apparently free, and she picks up her towels and rushes out)

MAMA What was they fighting about?

RUTH Now you know as well as I do.

MAMA *(Shaking her head)* Brother still worrying hisself sick about that money?

RUTH You know he is.

MAMA You had breakfast?

RUTH Some coffee.

MAMA Girl, you better start eating and looking after yourself better. You almost thin as Travis.

RUTH Lena—

MAMA Un-hunh?

RUTH What are you going to do with it?

MAMA Now don't you start, child. It's too early in the morning to be talking about money. It ain't Christian.

RUTH It's just that he got his heart set on that store—

MAMA You mean that liquor store that Willy Harris want him to invest in?

RUTH Yes—

MAMA We ain't no business people, Ruth. We just plain working folks.

RUTH Ain't nobody business people till they go into business. Walter Lee say colored people ain't never going to start getting ahead till they start gambling on some different kinds of things in the world—investments and things.

MAMA What done got into you, girl? Walter Lee done finally sold you on investing.

RUTH No. Mama, something is happening between Walter and me. I don't know what it is—but he needs something—something I can't give him anymore. He needs this chance, Lena.

MAMA *(Frowning deeply)* But liquor, honey—

RUTH Well—like Walter say—I spec people going to always be drinking themselves some liquor.

MAMA Well—whether they drinks it or not ain't none of my business. But whether I go into business selling it to 'em *is*, and I don't want that on my ledger this late in life. *(Stopping suddenly and studying her daughter-in-law)* Ruth Younger, what's the matter with you today? You look like you could fall over right there.

RUTH I'm tired.

MAMA Then you better stay home from work today.

RUTH I can't stay home. She'd be calling up the agency and screaming at them, "My girl didn't come in today— send me somebody! My girl didn't come in!" Oh, she just have a fit . . .

MAMA Well, let her have it. I'll just call her up and say you got the flu—

RUTH (*Laughing*) Why the flu?

MAMA 'Cause it sounds respectable to 'em. Something white people get, too. They know 'bout the flu. Otherwise they think you been cut up or something when you tell 'em you sick.

RUTH I got to go in. We need the money.

MAMA Somebody would of thought my children done all but starved to death the way they talk about money here late. Child, we got a great big old check coming tomorrow.

RUTH (*Sincerely, but also self-righteously*) Now that's your money. It ain't got nothing to do with me. We all feel like that—Walter and Bennie and me—even Travis.

MAMA (*Thoughtfully, and suddenly very far away*) Ten thousand dollars—

RUTH Sure is wonderful.

MAMA Ten thousand dollars.

RUTH You know what you should do, Miss Lena? You should take yourself a trip somewhere. To Europe or South America or someplace—

MAMA (*Throwing up her hands at the thought*) Oh, child!

RUTH I'm serious. Just pack up and leave! Go on away and enjoy yourself some. Forget about the family and have yourself a ball for once in your life—

MAMA (*Drily*) You sound like I'm just about ready to die. Who'd go with me? What I look like wandering 'round Europe by myself?

RUTH Shoot—these here rich white women do it all the time. They don't think nothing of packing up they suitcases and piling on one of them big steamships and—swoosh!—they gone, child.

MAMA Something always told me I wasn't no rich white woman.

RUTH Well—what are you going to do with it then?

MAMA I ain't rightly decided. *(Thinking. She speaks now with emphasis)* Some of it got to be put away for Beneatha and her schoolin'—and ain't nothing going to touch that part of it. Nothing. *(She waits several seconds, trying to make up her mind about something, and looks at* RUTH *a little tentatively before going on)* Been thinking that we maybe could meet the notes on a little old two-story somewhere, with a yard where Travis could play in the summertime, if we use part of the insurance for a down payment and everybody kind of pitch in. I could maybe take on a little day work again, few days a week—

RUTH *(Studying her mother-in-law furtively and concentrating on her ironing, anxious to encourage without seeming to)* Well, Lord knows, we've put enough rent into this here rat trap to pay for four houses by now . . .

MAMA *(Looking up at the words "rat trap" and then looking around and leaning back and sighing—in a suddenly reflective mood—)* "Rat trap"—yes, that's all it is. *(Smiling)* I remember just as well the day me and Big Walter moved in here. Hadn't been married but two weeks and wasn't planning on living here no more than a year. *(She shakes her head at the dissolved dream)* We was going to set away, little by little, don't you know, and buy a little place out in Morgan Park. We had even picked out the house. *(Chuckling a little)*

Looks right dumpy today. But Lord, child, you should know all the dreams I had 'bout buying that house and fixing it up and making me a little garden in the back— *(She waits and stops smiling)* And didn't none of it happen.

(Dropping her hands in a futile gesture)

RUTH *(Keeps her head down, ironing)* Yes, life can be a barrel of disappointments, sometimes.

MAMA Honey, Big Walter would come in here some nights back then and slump down on that couch there and just look at the rug, and look at me and look at the rug and then back at me—and I'd know he was down then . . . really down. *(After a second very long and thoughtful pause; she is seeing back to times that only she can see)* And then, Lord, when I lost that baby— little Claude—I almost thought I was going to lose Big Walter too. Oh, that man grieved hisself! He was one man to love his children.

RUTH Ain't nothin' can tear at you like losin' your baby.

MAMA I guess that's how come that man finally worked hisself to death like he done. Like he was fighting his own war with this here world that took his baby from him.

RUTH He sure was a fine man, all right. I always liked Mr. Younger.

MAMA Crazy 'bout his children! God knows there was plenty wrong with Walter Younger—hard-headed, mean, kind of wild with women—plenty wrong with him. But he sure loved his children. Always wanted them to have something—be something. That's where Brother gets all these notions, I reckon. Big Walter used to say, he'd get right wet in the eyes sometimes, lean his head back with the water standing in his eyes and say, "Seem like God didn't see fit to give the black man nothing but dreams—but He did give us children to make them dreams seem worth while." *(She smiles)* He could talk like that, don't you know.

RUTH Yes, he sure could. He was a good man, Mr. Younger.

MAMA Yes, a fine man—just couldn't never catch up with his dreams, that's all.
(BENEATHA *comes in, brushing her hair and looking up to the ceiling, where the sound of a vacuum cleaner has started up)*

BENEATHA What could be so dirty on that woman's rugs that she has to vacuum them every single day?

RUTH I wish certain young women 'round here who I could name would take inspiration about certain rugs in a certain apartment I could also mention.

BENEATHA *(Shrugging)* How much cleaning can a house need, for Christ's sakes.

MAMA *(Not liking the Lord's name used thus)* Bennie!

RUTH Just listen to her—just listen!

BENEATHA Oh, God!

MAMA If you use the Lord's name just one more time—

BENEATHA *(A bit of a whine)* Oh, Mama—

RUTH Fresh—just fresh as salt, this girl!

BENEATHA *(Drily)* Well—if the salt loses its savor—

MAMA Now that will do. I just ain't going to have you 'round here reciting the scriptures in vain—you hear me?

BENEATHA How did I manage to get on everybody's wrong side by just walking into a room?

RUTH If you weren't so fresh—

BENEATHA Ruth, I'm twenty years old.

MAMA What time you be home from school today?

BENEATHA Kind of late. (With enthusiasm) Madeline is going to start my guitar lessons today.
   (MAMA and RUTH look up with the same expression)

MAMA Your *what* kind of lessons?

BENEATHA Guitar.

RUTH Oh, Father!

MAMA How come you done taken it in your mind to learn to play the guitar?

BENEATHA I just want to, that's all.

MAMA (Smiling) Lord, child, don't you know what to do with yourself? How long it going to be before you get tired of this now—like you got tired of that little play-acting group you joined last year? (Looking at RUTH) And what was it the year before that?

RUTH The horseback-riding club for which she bought that fifty-five-dollar riding habit that's been hanging in the closet ever since!

MAMA (To BENEATHA) Why you got to flit so from one thing to another, baby?

BENEATHA (Sharply) I just want to learn to play the guitar. Is there anything wrong with that?

MAMA Ain't nobody trying to stop you. I just wonders sometimes why you has to flit so from one thing to another all the time. You ain't never done nothing with all that camera equipment you brought home—

BENEATHA I don't flit! I—I experiment with different forms of expression—

RUTH Like riding a horse?

BENEATHA —People have to express themselves one way or another.

MAMA What is it you want to express?

BENEATHA *(Angrily)* Me! *(MAMA and RUTH look at each other and burst into raucous laughter)* Don't worry—I don't expect you to understand.

MAMA *(To change the subject)* Who you going out with tomorrow night?

BENEATHA *(With displeasure)* George Murchison again.

MAMA *(Pleased)* Oh—you getting a little sweet on him?

RUTH You ask me, this child ain't sweet on nobody but herself—*(Underbreath)* Express herself!
  (They laugh)

BENEATHA Oh—I like George all right, Mama. I mean I like him enough to go out with him and stuff, but—

RUTH *(For devilment)* What does *and stuff* mean?

BENEATHA Mind your own business.

MAMA Stop picking at her now, Ruth. *(She chuckles— then a suspicious sudden look at her daughter as she turns in her chair for emphasis)* What DOES it mean?

BENEATHA *(Wearily)* Oh, I just mean I couldn't ever really be serious about George. He's—he's so shallow.

RUTH Shallow—what do you mean he's shallow? He's *rich!*

MAMA Hush, Ruth.

BENEATHA I know he's rich. He knows he's rich, too.

RUTH Well—what other qualities a man got to have to satisfy you, little girl?

BENEATHA You wouldn't even begin to understand. Anybody who married Walter could not possibly understand.

MAMA (*Outraged*) What kind of way is that to talk about your brother?

BENEATHA Brother is a flip—let's face it.

MAMA (*To* RUTH, *helplessly*) What's a flip?

RUTH (*Glad to add kindling*) She's saying he's crazy.

BENEATHA Not crazy. Brother isn't really crazy yet—he—he's an elaborate neurotic.

MAMA Hush your mouth!

BENEATHA As for George. Well. George looks good—he's got a beautiful car and he takes me to nice places and, as my sister-in-law says, he is probably the richest boy I will ever get to know and I even like him sometimes—but if the Youngers are sitting around waiting to see if their little Bennie is going to tie up the family with the Murchisons, they are wasting their time.

RUTH You mean you wouldn't marry George Murchison if he asked you someday? That pretty, rich thing? Honey, I knew you was odd—

BENEATHA No I would not marry him if all I felt for him was what I feel now. Besides, George's family wouldn't really like it.

MAMA Why not?

BENEATHA Oh, Mama—The Murchisons are honest-to-God-real-*live*-rich colored people, and the only people in the world who are more snobbish than rich white people are rich colored people. I thought everybody knew that. I've met Mrs. Murchison. She's a scene!

MAMA You must not dislike people 'cause they well off, honey.

BENEATHA Why not? It makes just as much sense as disliking people 'cause they are poor, and lots of people do that.

RUTH *(A wisdom-of-the-ages manner. To* MAMA*)* Well, she'll get over some of this—

BENEATHA Get over it? What are you talking about, Ruth? Listen, I'm going to be a doctor. I'm not worried about who I'm going to marry yet—if I ever get married.

MAMA *and* RUTH *If!*

MAMA Now, Bennie—

BENEATHA Oh, I probably will . . . but first I'm going to be a doctor, and George, for one, still thinks that's pretty funny. I couldn't be bothered with that. I am going to be a doctor and everybody around here better understand that!

MAMA *(Kindly)* 'Course you going to be a doctor, honey, God willing.

BENEATHA *(Drily)* God hasn't got a thing to do with it.

MAMA Beneatha—that just wasn't necessary.

BENEATHA Well—neither is God. I get sick of hearing about God.

MAMA Beneatha!

BENEATHA I mean it! I'm just tired of hearing about God all the time. What has He got to do with anything? Does he pay tuition?

MAMA You 'bout to get your fresh little jaw slapped!

RUTH That's just what she needs, all right!

BENEATHA Why? Why can't I say what I want to around here, like everybody else?

MAMA It don't sound nice for a young girl to say things like that—you wasn't brought up that way. Me and your father went to trouble to get you and Brother to church every Sunday.

BENEATHA Mama, you don't understand. It's all a matter of ideas, and God is just one idea I don't accept. It's not important. I am not going out and be immoral or commit crimes because I don't believe in God. I don't even think about it. It's just that I get tired of Him getting credit for all the things the human race achieves through its own stubborn effort. There simply is no blasted God— there is only man and it is *he* who makes miracles!
  (MAMA *absorbs this speech, studies her daughter and rises slowly and crosses to* BENEATHA *and slaps her powerfully across the face. After, there is only silence and the daughter drops her eyes from her mother's face, and* MAMA *is very tall before her*)

MAMA Now—you say after me, in my mother's house there is still God. (*There is a long pause and* BENEATHA *stares at the floor wordlessly.* MAMA *repeats the phrase with precision and cool emotion*) In my mother's house there is still God.

BENEATHA In my mother's house there is still God.
  (*A long pause*)

MAMA (*Walking away from* BENEATHA, *too disturbed for triumphant posture. Stopping and turning back to her daughter*) There are some ideas we ain't going to have in this house. Not long as I am at the head of this family.

BENEATHA Yes, ma'am.
　　(MAMA *walks out of the room*)

RUTH (*Almost gently, with profound understanding*) You think you a woman, Bennie—but you still a little girl. What you did was childish—so you got treated like a child.

BENEATHA I see. (*Quietly*) I also see that everybody thinks it's all right for Mama to be a tyrant. But all the tyranny in the world will never put a God in the heavens!
　　(*She picks up her books and goes out. Pause*)

RUTH (*Goes to* MAMA's *door*) She said she was sorry.

MAMA (*Coming out, going to her plant*) They frightens me, Ruth. My children.

RUTH You got good children, Lena. They just a little off sometimes—but they're good.

MAMA No—there's something come down between me and them that don't let us understand each other and I don't know what it is. One done almost lost his mind thinking 'bout money all the time and the other done commence to talk about things I can't seem to understand in no form or fashion. What is it that's changing, Ruth.

RUTH (*Soothingly, older than her years*) Now . . . you taking it all too seriously. You just got strong-willed children and it takes a strong woman like you to keep 'em in hand.

MAMA (*Looking at her plant and sprinkling a little water on it*) They spirited all right, my children. Got to admit they got spirit—Bennie and Walter. Like this little old plant that ain't never had enough sunshine or nothing—and look at it . . .

(She has her back to RUTH, *who has had to stop ironing and lean against something and put the back of her hand to her forehead)*

RUTH *(Trying to keep* MAMA *from noticing)* You . . . sure . . . loves that little old thing, don't you? . . .

MAMA Well, I always wanted me a garden like I used to see sometimes at the back of the houses down home. This plant is close as I ever got to having one. *(She looks out of the window as she replaces the plant)* Lord, ain't nothing as dreary as the view from this window on a dreary day, is there? Why ain't you singing this morning, Ruth? Sing that "No Ways Tired." That song always lifts me up so—*(She turns at last to see that* RUTH *has slipped quietly to the floor, in a state of semiconsciousness)* Ruth! Ruth honey—what's the matter with you . . . Ruth!

Curtain

SCENE TWO

It is the following morning; a Saturday morning, and house cleaning is in progress at the YOUNGERS. *Furniture has been shoved hither and yon and* MAMA *is giving the kitchen-area walls a washing down.* BENEATHA, *in dungarees, with a handkerchief tied around her face, is spraying insecticide into the cracks in the walls. As they work, the radio is on and a Southside disk-jockey program is inappropriately filling the house with a rather exotic saxophone blues.* TRAVIS, *the sole idle one, is leaning on his arms, looking out of the window.*

TRAVIS Grandmama, that stuff Bennie is using smells awful. Can I go downstairs, please?

MAMA Did you get all them chores done already? I ain't seen you doing much.

TRAVIS Yes'm—finished early. Where did Mama go this morning?

MAMA (*Looking at* BENEATHA) She had to go on a little errand.
     (*The phone rings.* BENEATHA *runs to answer it and reaches it before* WALTER, *who has entered from bedroom*)

TRAVIS Where?

MAMA To tend to her business.

BENEATHA Haylo . . . (*Disappointed*) Yes, he is. (*She tosses the phone to* WALTER, *who barely catches it*) It's Willie Harris again.

WALTER (*As privately as possible under* MAMA'S *gaze*)

Hello, Willie. Did you get the papers from the lawyer? . . . No, not yet. I told you the mailman doesn't get here till ten-thirty . . . No, I'll come there . . . Yeah! Right away. *(He hangs up and goes for his coat)*

BENEATHA Brother, where did Ruth go?

WALTER *(As he exits)* How should I know!

TRAVIS Aw come on, Grandma. Can I go outside?

MAMA Oh, I guess so. You stay right in front of the house, though, and keep a good lookout for the postman.

TRAVIS Yes'm. *(He darts into bedroom for stickball and bat, reenters, and sees* BENEATHA *on her knees spraying under sofa with behind upraised. He edges closer to the target, takes aim, and lets her have it. She screams)* Leave them poor little cockroaches alone, they ain't bothering you none! *(He runs as she swings the spray gun at him viciously and playfully)* Grandma! Grandma!

MAMA Look out there, girl, before you be spilling some of that stuff on that child!

TRAVIS *(Safely behind the bastion of* MAMA*)* That's right—look out, now! *(He exits)*

BENEATHA *(Drily)* I can't imagine that it would hurt him—it has never hurt the roaches.

MAMA Well, little boys' hides ain't as tough as Southside roaches. You better get over there behind the bureau. I seen one marching out of there like Napoleon yesterday.

BENEATHA There's really only one way to get rid of them, Mama—

MAMA How?

BENEATHA Set fire to this building! Mama, where did Ruth go?

MAMA *(Looking at her with meaning)* To the doctor, I think.

BENEATHA The doctor? What's the matter? *(They exchange glances)* You don't think—

MAMA *(With her sense of drama)* Now I ain't saying what I think. But I ain't never been wrong 'bout a woman neither.
(The phone rings)

BENEATHA *(At the phone)* Hay-lo . . . *(Pause, and a moment of recognition)* Well—when did you get back! . . . And how was it? . . . Of course I've missed you—in my way . . . This morning? No . . . house cleaning and all that and Mama hates it if I let people come over when the house is like this . . . You *have?* Well, that's different . . . What is it— Oh, what the hell, come on over . . . Right, see you then. *Arrivederci.*
(She hangs up)

MAMA *(Who has listened vigorously, as is her habit)* Who is that you inviting over here with this house looking like this? You ain't got the pride you was born with!

BENEATHA Asagai doesn't care how houses look, Mama—he's an intellectual.

MAMA *Who?*

BENEATHA Asagai—Joseph Asagai. He's an African boy I met on campus. He's been studying in Canada all summer.

MAMA What's his name?

BENEATHA Asagai, Joseph. Ah-sah-guy . . . He's from Nigeria.

MAMA Oh, that's the little country that was founded by slaves way back . . .

BENEATHA No, Mama—that's Liberia.

MAMA I don't think I never met no African before.

BENEATHA Well, do me a favor and don't ask him a whole lot of ignorant questions about Africans. I mean, do they wear clothes and all that—

MAMA Well, now, I guess if you think we so ignorant 'round here maybe you shouldn't bring your friends here—

BENEATHA It's just that people ask such crazy things. All anyone seems to know about when it comes to Africa is Tarzan—

MAMA (Indignantly) Why should I know anything about Africa?

BENEATHA Why do you give money at church for the missionary work?

MAMA Well, that's to help save people.

BENEATHA You mean save them from *heathenism*—

MAMA (Innocently) Yes.

BENEATHA I'm afraid they need more salvation from the British and the French.
(RUTH *comes in forlornly and pulls off her coat with dejection. They both turn to look at her*)

RUTH (Dispiritedly) Well, I guess from all the happy faces—everybody knows.

BENEATHA You pregnant?

MAMA Lord have mercy, I sure hope it's a little old girl. Travis ought to have a sister.
(BENEATHA *and* RUTH *give her a hopeless look for this grandmotherly enthusiasm*)

BENEATHA How far along are you?

RUTH Two months.

BENEATHA Did you mean to? I mean did you plan it or was it an accident?

MAMA What do you know about planning or not planning?

BENEATHA Oh, Mama.

RUTH *(Wearily)* She's twenty years old, Lena.

BENEATHA Did you plan it, Ruth?

RUTH Mind your own business.

BENEATHA It is my business—where is he going to live, on the *roof? (There is silence following the remark as the three women react to the sense of it)* Gee—I didn't mean that, Ruth, honest. Gee, I don't feel like that at all. I—I think it is wonderful.

RUTH *(Dully)* Wonderful.

BENEATHA Yes—really. *(There is a sudden commotion from the street and she goes to the window to look out)* What on earth is going on out there? These kids. *(There are, as she throws open the window, the shouts of children rising up from the street. She sticks her head out to see better and calls out)* TRAVIS! TRAVIS . . . WHAT ARE YOU DOING DOWN THERE? *(She sees)* Oh Lord, they're chasing a rat!
    (RUTH covers her face with hands and turns away)

MAMA *(Angrily)* Tell that youngun to get himself up here, at once!

BENEATHA TRAVIS . . . YOU COME UPSTAIRS . . . AT ONCE!

RUTH *(Her face twisted)* Chasing a rat. . . .

MAMA *(Looking at* RUTH, *worried)* Doctor say everything going to be all right?

RUTH *(Far away)* Yes—she says everything is going to be fine . . .

MAMA *(Immediately suspicious)* "She"—What doctor you went to?
>   *(*RUTH *just looks at* MAMA *meaningfully and* MAMA *opens her mouth to speak as* TRAVIS *bursts in)*

TRAVIS *(Excited and full of narrative, coming directly to his mother)* Mama, you should of seen the rat . . . Big as a cat, honest! *(He shows an exaggerated size with his hands)* Gaaleee, that rat was really cuttin' and Bubber caught him with his heel and the janitor, Mr. Barnett, got him with a stick—and then they got him in a corner and—BAM! BAM! BAM!—and he was still jumping around and bleeding like everything too—there's rat blood all over the street—
>   *(*RUTH *reaches out suddenly and grabs her son without even looking at him and clamps her hand over his mouth and holds him to her.* MAMA *crosses to them rapidly and takes the boy from her)*

MAMA You hush up now . . . talking all that terrible stuff. . . . *(*TRAVIS *is staring at his mother with a stunned expression.* BENEATHA *comes quickly and takes him away from his grandmother and ushers him to the door)*

BENEATHA You go back outside and play . . . but not with any rats. *(She pushes him gently out the door with the boy straining to see what is wrong with his mother)*

MAMA *(Worriedly hovering over* RUTH) Ruth honey— what's the matter with you—you sick?
>   *(*RUTH *has her fists clenched on her thighs and is fighting hard to suppress a scream that seems to be rising in her)*

BENEATHA What's the matter with her, Mama?

MAMA *(Working her fingers in* RUTH's *shoulders to relax her)* She be all right. Women gets right depressed sometimes when they get her way. *(Speaking softly, expertly, rapidly)* Now you just relax. That's right . . . just lean back, don't think 'bout nothing at all . . . nothing at all—

RUTH I'm all right . . .
    (The glassy-eyed look melts and then she collapses into a fit of heavy sobbing. The bell rings)

BENEATHA Oh, my God—that must be Asagai.

MAMA *(To* RUTH*)* Come on now, honey. You need to lie down and rest awhile . . . then have some nice hot food. *(They exit,* RUTH's *weight on her mother-in-law.* BENEATHA, *herself profoundly disturbed, opens the door to admit a rather dramatic-looking young man with a large package)*

ASAGAI Hello, Alaiyo—

BENEATHA *(Holding the door open and regarding him with pleasure)* Hello . . . *(Long pause)* Well—come in. And please excuse everything. My mother was very upset about my letting anyone come here with the place like this.

ASAGAI *(Coming into the room)* You look disturbed too . . . Is something wrong?

BENEATHA *(Still at the door, absently)* Yes . . . we've all got acute ghetto-itis. *(She smiles and comes toward him, finding a cigarette and sitting)* So—sit down! No! Wait! *(She whips the spray gun off sofa where she had left it and puts the cushions back. At last perches on arm of sofa. He sits)* So, how was Canada?

ASAGAI (*A sophisticate*) Canadian.

BENEATHA (*Looking at him*) Asagai, I'm very glad you are back.

ASAGAI (*Looking back at her in turn*) Are you really?

BENEATHA Yes—very.

ASAGAI Why?—you were quite glad when I went away. What happened?

BENEATHA You went away.

ASAGAI Ahhhhhhhh.

BENEATHA Before—you wanted to be so serious before there was time.

ASAGAI How much time must there be before one knows what one feels?

BENEATHA (*Stalling this particular conversation. Her hands pressed together, in a deliberately childish gesture*) What did you bring me?

ASAGAI (*Handing her the package*) Open it and see.

BENEATHA (*Eagerly opening the package and drawing out some records and the colorful robes of a Nigerian woman*) Oh, Asagai! . . . You got them for me! . . . How beautiful . . . and the records too! (*She lifts out the robes and runs to the mirror with them and holds the drapery up in front of herself*)

ASAGAI (*Coming to her at the mirror*) I shall have to teach you how to drape it properly. (*He flings the material about her for the moment and stands back to look at her*) Ah—Oh-pay-gay-day, oh-gbah-mu-shay. (*A Yoruba exclamation for admiration*) You wear it well . . . very well . . . mutilated hair and all.

BENEATHA (*Turning suddenly*) My hair—what's wrong with my hair?

ASAGAI *(Shrugging)* Were you born with it like that?

BENEATHA *(Reaching up to touch it)* No . . . of course not.
   (She looks back to the mirror, disturbed)

ASAGAI *(Smiling)* How then?

BENEATHA You know perfectly well how . . . as crinkly as yours . . . that's how.

ASAGAI And it is ugly to you that way?

BENEATHA *(Quickly)* Oh, no—not ugly . . . *(More slowly, apologetically)* But it's so hard to manage when it's, well—raw.

ASAGAI And so to accommodate that—you mutilate it every week?

BENEATHA It's not mutilation!

ASAGAI *(Laughing aloud at her seriousness)* Oh . . . please! I am only teasing you because you are so very serious about these things. *(He stands back from her and folds his arms across his chest as he watches her pulling at her hair and frowning in the mirror)* Do you remember the first time you met me at school? . . . *(He laughs)* You came up to me and you said—and I thought you were the most serious little thing I had ever seen—you said: *(He imitates her)* "Mr. Asagai—I want very much to talk with you. About Africa. You see, Mr. Asagai, I am looking for my *identity!*"
   (He laughs)

BENEATHA *(Turning to him, not laughing)* Yes—
   (Her face is quizzical, profoundly disturbed)

ASAGAI *(Still teasing and reaching out and taking her face in his hands and turning her profile to him)* Well . . . it is true that this is not so much a profile of a Hollywood queen as perhaps a queen of the Nile—*(A mock dismissal of the importance of the question)* But what does it matter? Assimilationism is so popular in your country.

BENEATHA *(Wheeling, passionately, sharply)* I am not an assimilationist!

ASAGAI *(The protest hangs in the room for a moment and* ASAGAI *studies her, his laughter fading)* Such a serious one. *(There is a pause)* So—you like the robes? You must take excellent care of them—they are from my sister's personal wardrobe.

BENEATHA *(With incredulity)* You—you sent all the way home—for me?

ASAGAI *(With charm)* For you—I would do much more . . . Well, that is what I came for. I must go.

BENEATHA Will you call me Monday?

ASAGAI Yes . . . We have a great deal to talk about. I mean about identity and time and all that.

BENEATHA Time?

ASAGAI Yes. About how much time one needs to know what one feels.

BENEATHA You see! You never understood that there is more than one kind of feeling which can exist between a man and a woman—or, at least, there should be.

ASAGAI *(Shaking his head negatively but gently)* No. Between a man and a woman there need be only one kind of feeling. I have that for you . . . Now even . . . right this moment . . .

BENEATHA I know—and by itself—it won't do. I can find that anywhere.

ASAGAI For a woman it should be enough.

BENEATHA I know—because that's what it says in all the
novels that men write. But it isn't. Go ahead and laugh—
but I'm not interested in being someone's little episode
in America or—(*With feminine vengeance*)—one of
them! (ASAGAI *has burst into laughter again*) That's funny
as hell, huh!

ASAGAI It's just that every American girl I have known
has said that to me. White—black—in this you are all
the same. And the same speech, too!

BENEATHA (*Angrily*) Yuk, yuk, yuk!

ASAGAI It's how you can be sure that the world's most
liberated women are not liberated at all. You all talk
about it too much!
  (MAMA *enters and is immediately all social charm because of the presence of a guest*)

BENEATHA Oh—Mama—this is Mr. Asagai.

MAMA How do you do?

ASAGAI (*Total politeness to an elder*) How do you do,
Mrs. Younger. Please forgive me for coming at such an
outrageous hour on a Saturday.

MAMA Well, you are quite welcome. I just hope you understand that our house don't always look like this.
(*Chatterish*) You must come again. I would love to hear
all about—(*Not sure of the name*)—your country. I think
it's so sad the way our American Negroes don't know
nothing about Africa 'cept Tarzan and all that. And all
that money they pour into these churches when they
ought to be helping you people over there drive out them
French and Englishmen done taken away your land.
  (*The mother flashes a slightly superior look at her
  daughter upon completion of the recitation*)

ASAGAI (*Taken aback by this sudden and acutely unrelated
expression of sympathy*) Yes . . . yes . . .

MAMA *(Smiling at him suddenly and relaxing and looking him over)* How many miles is it from here to where you come from?

ASAGAI Many thousands.

MAMA *(Looking at him as she would* WALTER*)* I bet you don't half look after yourself, being away from your mama either. I spec you better come 'round here from time to time to get yourself some decent home-cooked meals . . .

ASAGAI *(Moved)* Thank you. Thank you very much. *(They are all quiet, then—)* Well . . . I must go. I will call you Monday, Alaiyo.

MAMA What's that he call you?

ASAGAI Oh—"Alaiyo." I hope you don't mind. It is what you would call a nickname, I think. It is a Yoruba word. I am a Yoruba.

MAMA *(Looking at* BENEATHA*)* I—I thought he was from—*(Uncertain)*

ASAGAI *(Understanding)* Nigeria is my country. Yoruba is my tribal origin—

BENEATHA You didn't tell us what Alaiyo means . . . for all I know, you might be calling me Little Idiot or something . . .

ASAGAI Well . . . let me see . . . I do not know how just to explain it . . . The sense of a thing can be so different when it changes languages.

BENEATHA You're evading.

ASAGAI No—really it is difficult . . . *(Thinking)* It means . . . it means One for Whom Bread—Food—Is Not Enough. *(He looks at her)* Is that all right?

BENEATHA *(Understanding, softly)* Thank you.

MAMA (*Looking from one to the other and not under-standing any of it*) Well . . . that's nice . . . You must come see us again—Mr.——

ASAGAI Ah-sah-guy . . .

MAMA Yes . . . Do come again.

ASAGAI Good-bye.
(*He exits*)

MAMA (*After him*) Lord, that's a pretty thing just went out here! (*Insinuatingly, to her daughter*) Yes, I guess I see why we done commence to get so interested in Africa 'round here. Missionaries my aunt Jenny!
(*She exits*)

BENEATHA Oh, Mama! . . .
(*She picks up the Nigerian dress and holds it up to her in front of the mirror again. She sets the headdress on haphazardly and then notices her hair again and clutches at it and then replaces the headdress and frowns at herself. Then she starts to wriggle in front of the mirror as she thinks a Nigerian woman might.* TRAVIS *enters and stands regarding her*)

TRAVIS What's the matter, girl, you cracking up?

BENEATHA Shut up.
(*She pulls the headdress off and looks at herself in the mirror and clutches at her hair again and squinches her eyes as if trying to imagine something. Then, suddenly, she gets her raincoat and kerchief and hurriedly prepares for going out*)

MAMA (*Coming back into the room*) She's resting now. Travis, baby, run next door and ask Miss Johnson to please let me have a little kitchen cleanser. This here can is empty as Jacob's kettle.

TRAVIS I just came in.

MAMA Do as you told. *(He exits and she looks at her daughter)* Where you going?

BENEATHA *(Halting at the door)* To become a queen of the Nile!
  (She exits in a breathless blaze of glory. RUTH *appears in the bedroom doorway)*

MAMA Who told you to get up?

RUTH Ain't nothing wrong with me to be lying in no bed for. Where did Bennie go?

MAMA *(Drumming her fingers)* Far as I could make out— to Egypt. (RUTH *just looks at her)* What time is it getting to?

RUTH Ten twenty. And the mailman going to ring that bell this morning just like he done every morning for the last umpteen years.
  (TRAVIS *comes in with the cleanser can)*

TRAVIS She say to tell you that she don't have much.

MAMA *(Angrily)* Lord, some people I could name sure is tight-fisted! *(Directing her grandson)* Mark two cans of cleanser down on the list there. If she that hard up for kitchen cleanser, I sure don't want to forget to get her none!

RUTH Lena—maybe the woman is just short on cleanser—

MAMA *(Not listening)*—Much baking powder as she done borrowed from me all these years, she could of done gone into the baking business!
  (The bell sounds suddenly and sharply and all three are stunned—serious and silent—mid-speech. In spite of all the other conversations and distractions of the morning, this is what they have

been waiting for, even TRAVIS *who looks helplessly
from his mother to his grandmother.* RUTH *is the first
to come to life again)*

RUTH *(To* TRAVIS*)* Get down them steps, boy!
(TRAVIS *snaps to life and flies out to get the mail)*

MAMA *(Her eyes wide, her hand to her breast)* You mean
it done really come?

RUTH *(Excited)* Oh, Miss Lena!

MAMA *(Collecting herself)* Well . . . I don't know what we
all so excited about 'round here for. We known it was
coming for months.

RUTH That's a whole lot different from having it come
and being able to hold it in your hands . . . a piece of
paper worth ten thousand dollars . . . (TRAVIS *bursts
back into the room. He holds the envelope high above
his head, like a little dancer, his face is radiant and he is
breathless. He moves to his grandmother with sudden
slow ceremony and puts the envelope into her hands. She
accepts it, and then merely holds it and looks at it)* Come
on! Open it . . . Lord have mercy, I wish Walter Lee was
here!

TRAVIS Open it, Grandmama!

MAMA *(Staring at it)* Now you all be quiet. It's just a check.

RUTH Open it . . .

MAMA *(Still staring at it)* Now don't act silly . . . We ain't
never been no people to act silly 'bout no money—

RUTH *(Swiftly)* We ain't never had none before—OPEN
IT!
(MAMA *finally makes a good strong tear and pulls
out the thin blue slice of paper and inspects it*

closely. The boy and his mother study it raptly over
MAMA's *shoulders)*

MAMA Travis! *(She is counting off with doubt)* Is that the
right number of zeros?

TRAVIS Yes'm . . . ten thousand dollars. Gaalee, Grandmama, you rich.

MAMA *(She holds the check away from her, still looking
at it. Slowly her face sobers into a mask of unhappi-
ness)* Ten thousand dollars. *(She hands it to* RUTH*)* Put
it away somewhere, Ruth. *(She does not look at* RUTH;
*her eyes seem to be seeing something somewhere very
far off)* Ten thousand dollars they give you. Ten thousand dollars.

TRAVIS *(To his mother, sincerely)* What's the matter with
Grandmama—don't she want to be rich?

RUTH *(Distractedly)* You go on out and play now, baby.
*(*TRAVIS *exits.* MAMA *starts wiping dishes absently, hum-
ming intently to herself.* RUTH *turns to her, with kind
exasperation)* You've gone and got yourself upset.

MAMA *(Not looking at her)* I spec if it wasn't for you
all . . . I would just put that money away or give it to the
church or something.

RUTH Now what kind of talk is that. Mr. Younger would
just be plain mad if he could hear you talking foolish
like that.

MAMA *(Stopping and staring off)* Yes . . . he sure would.
(Sighing) We got enough to do with that money, all right.
*(She halts then, and turns and looks at her daughter-in-
law hard;* RUTH *avoids her eyes and* MAMA *wipes her
hands with finality and starts to speak firmly to* RUTH*)*
Where did you go today, girl?

RUTH To the doctor.

MAMA *(Impatiently)* Now, Ruth . . . you know better than that. Old Doctor Jones is strange enough in his way but there ain't nothing 'bout him make somebody slip and call him "she"—like you done this morning.

RUTH Well, that's what happened—my tongue slipped.

MAMA You went to see that woman, didn't you?

RUTH *(Defensively, giving herself away)* What woman you talking about?

MAMA *(Angrily)* That woman who—
   (WALTER enters in great excitement)

WALTER Did it come?

MAMA *(Quietly)* Can't you give people a Christian greeting before you start asking about money?

WALTER *(To RUTH)* Did it come? *(RUTH unfolds the check and lays it quietly before him, watching him intently with thoughts of her own. WALTER sits down and grasps it close and counts off the zeros)* Ten thousand dollars—*(He turns suddenly, frantically to his mother and draws some papers out of his breast pocket)* Mama—look. Old Willy Harris put everything on paper—

MAMA Son—I think you ought to talk to your wife . . . I'll go on out and leave you alone if you want—

WALTER I can talk to her later—Mama, look—

MAMA Son—

WALTER WILL SOMEBODY PLEASE LISTEN TO ME TODAY!

MAMA *(Quietly)* I don't 'low no yellin' in this house, Walter Lee, and you know it—*(WALTER stares at them in frustration and starts to speak several times)* And there ain't going to be no investing in no liquor stores.

WALTER But, Mama, you ain't even looked at it.

MAMA I don't aim to have to speak on that again.
 (A long pause)

WALTER You ain't looked at it and you don't aim to have
 to speak on that again? You ain't even looked at it and
 you have decided—*(Crumpling his papers)* Well, *you* tell
 that to my boy tonight when you put him to sleep on the
 living-room couch . . . *(Turning to* MAMA *and speaking
 directly to her)* Yeah—and tell it to my wife, Mama, tomorrow when she has to go out of here to look after somebody
 else's kids. And tell it to *me*, Mama, every time we need
 a new pair of curtains and I have to watch *you* go out
 and work in somebody's kitchen. Yeah, you tell me then!
 (WALTER starts out)

RUTH Where you going?

WALTER I'm going out!

RUTH Where?

WALTER Just out of this house somewhere—

RUTH *(Getting her coat)* I'll come too.

WALTER I don't want you to come!

RUTH I got something to talk to you about, Walter.

WALTER That's too bad.

MAMA *(Still quietly)* Walter Lee—*(She waits and he finally
 turns and looks at her)* Sit down.

WALTER I'm a grown man, Mama.

MAMA Ain't nobody said you wasn't grown. But you still
 in my house and my presence. And as long as you are—
 you'll talk to your wife civil. Now sit down.

RUTH *(Suddenly)* Oh, let him go on out and drink himself
 to death! He makes me sick to my stomach! *(She flings
 her coat against him and exits to bedroom)*

WALTER *(Violently flinging the coat after her)* And you turn mine too, baby! *(The door slams behind her)* That was my biggest mistake—

MAMA *(Still quietly)* Walter, what is the matter with you?

WALTER Matter with me? Ain't nothing the matter with *me!*

MAMA Yes there is. Something eating you up like a crazy man. Something more than me not giving you this money. The past few years I been watching it happen to you. You get all nervous acting and kind of wild in the eyes— *(WALTER jumps up impatiently at her words)* I said sit there now, I'm talking to you!

WALTER Mama—I don't need no nagging at me today.

MAMA Seem like you getting to a place where you always tied up in some kind of knot about something. But if anybody ask you 'bout it you just yell at 'em and bust out the house and go out and drink somewheres. Walter Lee, people can't live with that. Ruth's a good, patient girl in her way—but you getting to be too much. Boy, don't make the mistake of driving that girl away from you.

WALTER Why—what she do for me?

MAMA She loves you.

WALTER Mama—I'm going out. I want to go off somewhere and be by myself for a while.

MAMA I'm sorry 'bout your liquor store, son. It just wasn't the thing for us to do. That's what I want to tell you about—

WALTER I got to go out, Mama—
(He rises)

MAMA It's dangerous, son.

WALTER What's dangerous?

MAMA When a man goes outside his home to look for peace.

WALTER (*Beseechingly*) Then why can't there never be no peace in this house then?

MAMA You done found it in some other house?

WALTER No—there ain't no woman! Why do women always think there's a woman somewhere when a man gets restless. (*Picks up the check*) Do you know what this money means to me? Do you know what this money can do for us? (*Puts it back*) Mama—Mama—I want so many things . . .

MAMA Yes, son—

WALTER I want so many things that they are driving me kind of crazy . . . Mama—look at me.

MAMA I'm looking at you. You a good-looking boy. You got a job, a nice wife, a fine boy and—

WALTER A job. (*Looks at her*) Mama, a job? I open and close car doors all day long. I drive a man around in his limousine and I say, "Yes, sir; no, sir; very good, sir; shall I take the Drive, sir?" Mama, that ain't no kind of job . . . that ain't nothing at all. (*Very quietly*) Mama, I don't know if I can make you understand.

MAMA Understand what, baby?

WALTER (*Quietly*) Sometimes it's like I can see the future stretched out in front of me—just plain as day. The future, Mama. Hanging over there at the edge of my days. Just waiting for me—a big, looming blank space—full of *nothing*. Just waiting for *me*. But it don't have to be. *(Pause. Kneeling beside her chair)* Mama—sometimes when I'm downtown and I pass them cool, quiet-looking restaurants where them white boys are sitting back and talking 'bout things . . . sitting there turning deals worth millions of dollars . . . sometimes I see guys don't look much older than me—

MAMA Son—how come you talk so much 'bout money?

WALTER *(With immense passion)* Because it is life, Mama!

MAMA *(Quietly)* Oh—*(Very quietly)* So now it's life. Money is life. Once upon a time freedom used to be life—now it's money. I guess the world really do change . . .

WALTER No—it was always money, Mama. We just didn't know about it.

MAMA No . . . something has changed. *(She looks at him)* You something new, boy. In my time we was worried about not being lynched and getting to the North if we could and how to stay alive and still have a pinch of dignity too . . . Now here come you and Beneatha—talking 'bout things we ain't never even thought about hardly, me and your daddy. You ain't satisfied or proud of nothing we done. I mean that you had a home; that we kept you out of trouble till you was grown; that you don't have to ride to work on the back of nobody's streetcar— You my children—but how different we done become.

WALTER *(A long beat. He pats her hand and gets up)* You just don't understand, Mama, you just don't understand.

MAMA Son—do you know your wife is expecting another baby? *(WALTER stands, stunned, and absorbs what his mother has said)* That's what she wanted to talk to you about. (WALTER *sinks down into a chair*) This ain't for me to be telling—but you ought to know. *(She waits)* I think Ruth is thinking 'bout getting rid of that child.

WALTER *(Slowly understanding)* No—no—Ruth wouldn't do that.

MAMA When the world gets ugly enough—a woman will do anything for her family. *The part that's already living.*

WALTER You don't know Ruth, Mama, if you think she would do that.

(RUTH *opens the bedroom door and stands there a little limp)*

RUTH *(Beaten)* Yes I would too, Walter. *(Pause)* I gave her a five-dollar down payment.

(There is total silence as the man stares at his wife and the mother stares at her son)

MAMA *(Presently)* Well — *(Tightly)* Well — son, I'm waiting to hear you say something . . . *(She waits)* I'm waiting to hear how you be your father's son. Be the man he was . . . *(Pause. The silence shouts)* Your wife say she going to destroy your child. And I'm waiting to hear you talk like him and say we a people who give children life, not who destroys them—*(She rises)* I'm waiting to see you stand up and look like your daddy and say we done give up one baby to poverty and that we ain't going to give up nary another one . . . I'm waiting.

WALTER Ruth— *(He can say nothing)*

MAMA If you a son of mine, tell her! (WALTER *picks up his keys and his coat and walks out. She continues, bitterly)* You . . . you are a disgrace to your father's memory. Somebody get me my hat!

Curtain

ACT II

SCENE ONE

Time: Later the same day.

At rise: RUTH *is ironing again. She has the radio going. Presently* BENEATHA'S *bedroom door opens and* RUTH'S *mouth falls and she puts down the iron in fascination.*

RUTH What have we got on tonight!

BENEATHA *(Emerging grandly from the doorway so that we can see her thoroughly robed in the costume Asagai brought)* You are looking at what a well-dressed Nigerian woman wears—*(She parades for* RUTH, *her hair completely hidden by the headdress; she is coquettishly fanning herself with an ornate oriental fan, mistakenly more like Butterfly than any Nigerian that ever was)* Isn't it beautiful? *(She promenades to the radio and, with an arrogant flourish, turns off the good loud blues that is playing)* Enough of this assimilationist junk! *(*RUTH *follows her with her eyes as she goes to the phonograph and puts on a record and turns and waits ceremoniously for the music to come up. Then, with a shout—)* OCOMOGOSIAY!

  *(*RUTH *jumps. The music comes up, a lovely Nigerian melody.* BENEATHA *listens, enraptured, her*

eyes far away—"back to the past." She begins to dance.
RUTH *is dumbfounded)*

RUTH What kind of dance is that?

BENEATHA A folk dance.

RUTH *(Pearl Bailey)* What kind of folks do that, honey?

BENEATHA It's from Nigeria. It's a dance of welcome.

RUTH Who you welcoming?

BENEATHA The men back to the village.

RUTH Where they been?

BENEATHA How should I know—out hunting or something. Anyway, they are coming back now . . .

RUTH Well, that's good.

BENEATHA *(With the record)*
Alundi, alundi
Alundi alunya
Jop pu a jeepua
Ang gu soooooooooGo

Ai yai yae . . .
Ayehaye—alundi . . .
   (WALTER comes in during this performance; he has obviously been drinking. He leans against the door heavily and watches his sister, at first with distaste. Then his eyes look off—"back to the past"—as he lifts both his fists to the roof, screaming)

WALTER YEAH . . . AND ETHIOPIA STRETCH FORTH HER HANDS AGAIN! . . .

RUTH *(Drily, looking at him)* Yes—and Africa sure is claiming her own tonight. *(She gives them both up and starts ironing again)*

WALTER *(All in a drunken, dramatic shout)* Shut up! ... I'm digging them drums ... them drums move me! ... *(He makes his weaving way to his wife's face and leans in close to her)* In my *heart of hearts—(He thumps his chest)*—I am much warrior!

RUTH *(Without even looking up)* In your heart of hearts you are much drunkard.

WALTER *(Coming away from her and starting to wander around the room, shouting)* Me and Jomo ... *(Intently, in his sister's face. She has stopped dancing to watch him in this unknown mood)* That's my man, Kenyatta. *(Shouting and thumping his chest)* FLAMING SPEAR! HOT DAMN! *(He is suddenly in possession of an imaginary spear and actively spearing enemies all over the room)* OCOMOGOSIAY ...

BENEATHA *(To encourage WALTER, thoroughly caught up with this side of him)* OCOMOGOSIAY, FLAMING SPEAR!

WALTER THE LION IS WAKING ... OWIMOWEH! *(He pulls his shirt open and leaps up on the table and gestures with his spear)*

BENEATHA OWIMOWEH!

WALTER *(On the table, very far gone, his eyes pure glass sheets. He sees what we cannot, that he is a leader of his people, a great chief, a descendant of Chaka, and that the hour to march has come)* Listen, my black brothers—

BENEATHA OCOMOGOSIAY!

WALTER —Do you hear the waters rushing against the shores of the coastlands—

BENEATHA OCOMOGOSIAY!

WALTER —Do you hear the screeching of the cocks in yonder hills beyond where the chiefs meet in council for the coming of the mighty war—

BENEATHA OCOMOGOSIAY!
(And now the lighting shifts subtly to suggest the world of WALTER'S *imagination, and the mood shifts from pure comedy. It is the inner* WALTER *speaking: the Southside chauffeur has assumed an unexpected majesty)*

WALTER —Do you hear the beating of the wings of the birds flying low over the mountains and the low places of our land—

BENEATHA OCOMOGOSIAY!

WALTER —Do you hear the singing of the women, singing the war songs of our fathers to the babies in the great houses? Singing the sweet war songs! *(The doorbell rings)* OH, DO YOU HEAR, MY BLACK BROTHERS!

BENEATHA *(Completely gone)* We hear you, Flaming Spear—
*(*RUTH *shuts off the phonograph and opens the door.* GEORGE MURCHISON *enters)*

WALTER Telling us to prepare for the GREATNESS OF THE TIME! *(Lights back to normal. He turns and sees* GEORGE*)* Black Brother!
(He extends his hand for the fraternal clasp)

GEORGE Black Brother, hell!

RUTH *(Having had enough, and embarrassed for the family)* Beneatha, you got company—what's the matter with you? Walter Lee Younger, get down off that table and stop acting like a fool . . .

(WALTER comes down off the table suddenly and makes a quick exit to the bathroom)

RUTH He's had a little to drink . . . I don't know what her excuse is.

GEORGE *(To BENEATHA)* Look honey, we're going *to* the theatre—we're not going to be *in* it . . . so go change, huh?
(BENEATHA looks at him and slowly, ceremoniously, lifts her hands and pulls off the headdress. Her hair is close-cropped and unstraightened. GEORGE freezes mid-sentence and RUTH'S eyes all but fan out of her head)

GEORGE What in the name of—

RUTH *(Touching BENEATHA'S hair)* Girl, you done lost your natural mind!? Look at your head!

GEORGE What have you done to your head—I mean your hair!

BENEATHA Nothing—except cut it off.

RUTH Now that's the truth—it's what ain't been done to it! You expect this boy to go out with you with your head all nappy like that?

BENEATHA *(Looking at GEORGE)* That's up to George. If he's ashamed of his heritage—

GEORGE Oh, don't be so proud of yourself, Bennie—just because you look eccentric.

BENEATHA How can something that's natural be eccentric?

GEORGE That's what being eccentric means—being natural. Get dressed.

BENEATHA I don't like that, George.

RUTH Why must you and your brother make an argument out of everything people say?

BENEATHA Because I hate assimilationist Negroes!

RUTH Will somebody please tell me what assimila-who-ever means!

GEORGE Oh, it's just a college girl's way of calling people Uncle Toms—but that isn't what it means at all.

RUTH Well, what does it mean?

BENEATHA *(Cutting* GEORGE *off and staring at him as she replies to* RUTH*)* It means someone who is willing to give up his own culture and submerge himself completely in the dominant, and in this case *oppressive* culture!

GEORGE Oh, dear, dear, dear! Here we go! A lecture on the African past! On our Great West African Heritage! In one second we will hear all about the great Ashanti empires; the great Songhay civilizations; and the great sculpture of Bénin—and then some poetry in the Bantu—and the whole monologue will end with the word *heritage! (Nastily)* Let's face it, baby, your heritage is nothing but a bunch of raggedy-assed spirituals and some grass huts!

BENEATHA GRASS HUTS! *(RUTH crosses to her and forcibly pushes her toward the bedroom)* See there . . . you are standing there in your splendid ignorance talking about people who were the first to smelt iron on the face of the earth! *(RUTH is pushing her through the door)* The Ashanti were performing surgical operations when the English—*(RUTH pulls the door to, with BENEATHA on the other side, and smiles graciously at GEORGE. BENEATHA opens the door and shouts the end of the sentence defiantly at GEORGE)*—were still tattooing themselves with blue dragons! *(She goes back inside)*

RUTH Have a seat, George *(They both sit.* RUTH *folds her hands rather primly on her lap, determined to demonstrate the civilization of the family)* Warm, ain't it? I mean for September. *(Pause)* Just like they always say about Chicago weather: If it's too hot or cold for you, just wait a minute and it'll change. *(She smiles happily at this cliché of clichés)* Everybody say it's got to do with them bombs and things they keep setting off. *(Pause)* Would you like a nice cold beer?

GEORGE No, thank you. I don't care for beer. *(He looks at his watch)* I hope she hurries up.

RUTH What time is the show?

GEORGE It's an eight-thirty curtain. That's just Chicago, though. In New York standard curtain time is eight forty. *(He is rather proud of this knowledge)*

RUTH *(Properly appreciating it)* You get to New York a lot?

GEORGE *(Offhand)* Few times a year.

RUTH Oh—that's nice. I've never been to New York. *(WALTER enters. We feel he has relieved himself, but the edge of unreality is still with him)*

WALTER New York ain't got nothing Chicago ain't. Just a bunch of hustling people all squeezed up together— being "Eastern."
(He turns his face into a screw of displeasure)

GEORGE Oh—you've been?

WALTER *Plenty* of times.

RUTH *(Shocked at the lie)* Walter Lee Younger!

WALTER *(Staring her down)* Plenty! *(Pause)* What we got to drink in this house? Why don't you offer this man some refreshment. *(To* GEORGE*)* They don't know how to entertain people in this house, man.

GEORGE Thank you—I don't really care for anything.

WALTER *(Feeling his head; sobriety coming)* Where's Mama?

RUTH She ain't come back yet.

WALTER *(Looking* MURCHISON *over from head to toe, scrutinizing his carefully casual tweed sports jacket over cashmere V-neck sweater over soft eyelet shirt and tie, and soft slacks, finished off with white buckskin shoes)* Why all you college boys wear them faggoty-looking white shoes?

RUTH Walter Lee!
    *(*GEORGE MURCHISON *ignores the remark)*

WALTER *(To* RUTH*)* Well, they look crazy as hell—white shoes, cold as it is.

RUTH *(Crushed)* You have to excuse him—

WALTER No he don't! Excuse me for what? What you always excusing me for! I'll excuse myself when I needs to be excused! *(A pause)* They look as funny as them black knee socks Beneatha wears out of here all the time.

RUTH It's the college *style,* Walter.

WALTER Style, hell. She looks like she got burnt legs or something!

RUTH Oh, Walter—

WALTER *(An irritable mimic)* Oh, Walter! Oh, Walter! *(To* MURCHISON*)* How's your old man making out? I understand you all going to buy that big hotel on the Drive? *(He finds a beer in the refrigerator, wanders over to* MURCHISON, *sipping and wiping his lips with*

*the back of his hand, and straddling a chair backwards
to talk to the other man)* Shrewd move. Your old man
is all right, man. *(Tapping his head and half winking for
emphasis)* I mean he knows how to operate. I mean he
thinks *big,* you know what I mean, I mean for a *home,*
you know? But I think he's kind of running out of ideas
now. I'd like to talk to him. Listen, man, I got some plans
that could turn this city upside down. I mean think like
he does. *Big.* Invest big, gamble big, hell, lose *big* if you
have to, you know what I mean. It's hard to find a man
on this whole Southside who understands my kind of
thinking—you dig? *(He scrutinizes* MURCHISON *again,
drinks his beer, squints his eyes and leans in close, con-
fidential, man to man)* Me and you ought to sit down
and talk sometimes, man. Man, I got me some ideas . . .

GEORGE *(With boredom)* Yeah—sometimes we'll have to
do that, Walter.

WALTER *(Understanding the indifference, and offended)*
Yeah—well, when you get the time, man. I know you a
busy little boy.

RUTH Walter, please—

WALTER *(Bitterly, hurt)* I know ain't nothing in this world
as busy as you colored college boys with your fraternity
pins and white shoes . . .

RUTH *(Covering her face with humiliation)* Oh, Walter
Lee—

WALTER I see you all all the time—with the books
tucked under your arms—going to your *(British A—a
mimic)* "clahsses." And for what! What the hell you
learning over there? Filling up your heads—*(Counting off on his fingers)*—with the sociology and the
psychology—but they teaching you how to be a man?

How to take over and run the world? They teaching you how to run a rubber plantation or a steel mill? Naw— just to talk proper and read books and wear them faggoty-looking white shoes . . .

GEORGE (*Looking at him with distaste, a little above it all*) You're all wacked up with bitterness, man.

WALTER (*Intently, almost quietly, between the teeth, glaring at the boy*) And you—ain't you bitter, man? Ain't you just about had it yet? Don't you see no stars gleaming that you can't reach out and grab? You happy?—You contented son-of-a-bitch—you happy? You got it made? Bitter? Man, I'm a volcano. Bitter? Here I am a giant— surrounded by ants! Ants who can't even understand what it is the giant is talking about.

RUTH (*Passionately and suddenly*) Oh, Walter—ain't you with nobody!

WALTER (*Violently*) No! 'Cause ain't nobody with me! Not even my own mother!

RUTH Walter, that's a terrible thing to say!
(BENEATHA *enters, dressed for the evening in a cocktail dress and earrings, hair natural*)

GEORGE Well—hey—(*Crosses to* BENEATHA; *thoughtful, with emphasis, since this is a reversal*) You look great!

WALTER (*Seeing his sister's hair for the first time*) What's the matter with your head?

BENEATHA (*Tired of the jokes now*) I cut it off, Brother.

WALTER (*Coming close to inspect it and walking around her*) Well, I'll be damned. So that's what they mean by the African bush . . .

BENEATHA Ha ha. Let's go, George.

GEORGE *(Looking at her)* You know something? I like it. It's sharp. I mean it really is. *(Helps her into her wrap)*

RUTH Yes—I think so, too. *(She goes to the mirror and starts to clutch at her hair)*

WALTER Oh no! You leave yours alone, baby. You might turn out to have a pin-shaped head or something!

BENEATHA See you all later.

RUTH Have a nice time.

GEORGE Thanks. Good night. *(Half out the door, he re-opens it. To* WALTER*)* Good night, Prometheus!
    *(*BENEATHA *and* GEORGE *exit)*

WALTER *(To* RUTH*)* Who is Prometheus?

RUTH I don't know. Don't worry about it.

WALTER *(In fury, pointing after* GEORGE*)* See there—they get to a point where they can't insult you man to man— they got to go talk about something ain't nobody never heard of!

RUTH How do you know it was an insult? *(To humor him)* Maybe Prometheus is a nice fellow.

WALTER Prometheus! I bet there ain't even no such thing! I bet that simple-minded clown—

RUTH Walter—
    (She stops what she is doing and looks at him)

WALTER *(Yelling)* Don't start!

RUTH Start what?

WALTER Your nagging! Where was I? Who was I with? How much money did I spend?

RUTH *(Plaintively)* Walter Lee—why don't we just try to talk about it . . .

WALTER *(Not listening)* I been out talking with people who understand me. People who care about the things I got on my mind.

RUTH *(Wearily)* I guess that means people like Willy Harris.

WALTER Yes, people like Willy Harris.

RUTH *(With a sudden flash of impatience)* Why don't you all just hurry up and go into the banking business and stop talking about it!

WALTER Why? You want to know why? 'Cause we all tied up in a race of people that don't know how to do nothing but moan, pray and have babies!
(The line is too bitter even for him and he looks at her and sits down)

RUTH Oh, Walter . . . *(Softly)* Honey, why can't you stop fighting me?

WALTER *(Without thinking)* Who's fighting you? Who even cares about you?
(This line begins the retardation of his mood)

RUTH Well—*(She waits a long time, and then with resignation starts to put away her things)* I guess I might as well go on to bed . . . *(More or less to herself)* I don't know where we lost it . . . but we have . . . *(Then, to him)* I—I'm sorry about this new baby, Walter. I guess maybe I better go on and do what I started . . . I guess I just didn't realize how bad things was with us . . . I guess I just didn't really realize—*(She starts out to the bedroom and stops)* You want some hot milk?

WALTER Hot milk?

RUTH Yes—hot milk.

WALTER Why hot milk?

RUTH 'Cause after all that liquor you come home with you ought to have something hot in your stomach.

WALTER I don't want no milk.

RUTH You want some coffee then?

WALTER No, I don't want no coffee. I don't want nothing hot to drink. *(Almost plaintively)* Why you always trying to give me something to eat?

RUTH *(Standing and looking at him helplessly)* What else can I give you, Walter Lee Younger?
(She stands and looks at him and presently turns to go out again. He lifts his head and watches her going away from him in a new mood which began to emerge when he asked her "Who cares about you?")

WALTER It's been rough, ain't it, baby? *(She hears and stops but does not turn around and he continues to her back)* I guess between two people there ain't never as much understood as folks generally thinks there is. I mean like between me and you—*(She turns to face him)* How we gets to the place where we scared to talk softness to each other. *(He waits, thinking hard himself)* Why you think it got to be like that? *(He is thoughtful, almost as a child would be)* Ruth, what is it gets into people ought to be close?

RUTH I don't know, honey. I think about it a lot.

WALTER On account of you and me, you mean? The way things are with us. The way something done come down between us.

RUTH There ain't so much between us, Walter . . . Not when you come to me and try to talk to me. Try to be with me . . . a little even.

WALTER *(Total honesty)* Sometimes . . . sometimes . . . I don't even know how to try.

RUTH Walter—

WALTER Yes?

RUTH *(Coming to him, gently and with misgiving, but coming to him)* Honey . . . life don't have to be like this. I mean sometimes people can do things so that things are better . . . You remember how we used to talk when Travis was born . . . about the way we were going to live . . . the kind of house . . . *(She is stroking his head)* Well, it's all starting to slip away from us . . .
  (He turns her to him and they look at each other and kiss, tenderly and hungrily. The door opens and MAMA *enters—*WALTER *breaks away and jumps up. A beat)*

WALTER Mama, where have you been?

MAMA My—them steps is longer than they used to be. Whew! *(She sits down and ignores him)* How you feeling this evening, Ruth?
  *(*RUTH *shrugs, disturbed at having been interrupted and watching her husband knowingly)*

WALTER Mama, where have you been all day?

MAMA *(Still ignoring him and leaning on the table and changing to more comfortable shoes)* Where's Travis?

RUTH I let him go out earlier and he ain't come back yet. Boy, is he going to get it!

WALTER Mama!

MAMA *(As if she has heard him for the first time)* Yes, son?

WALTER Where did you go this afternoon?

MAMA I went downtown to tend to some business that I had to tend to.

WALTER What kind of business?

MAMA You know better than to question me like a child, Brother.

WALTER (*Rising and bending over the table*) Where were you, Mama? (*Bringing his fists down and shouting*) Mama, you didn't go do something with that insurance money, something crazy?
    (*The front door opens slowly, interrupting him, and* TRAVIS *peeks his head in, less than hopefully*)

TRAVIS (*To his mother*) Mama, I—

RUTH "Mama I" nothing! You're going to get it, boy! Get on in that bedroom and get yourself ready!

TRAVIS But I—

MAMA Why don't you all never let the child explain hisself.

RUTH Keep out of it now, Lena.
    (MAMA *clamps her lips together, and* RUTH *advances toward her son menacingly*)

RUTH A thousand times I have told you not to go off like that—

MAMA (*Holding out her arms to her grandson*) Well—at least let me tell him something. I want him to be the first one to hear . . . Come here, Travis. (*The boy obeys, gladly*) Travis—(*She takes him by the shoulder and looks into his face*)—you know that money we got in the mail this morning?

TRAVIS Yes'm—

MAMA Well—what you think your grandmama gone and done with that money?

TRAVIS I don't know, Grandmama.

MAMA *(Putting her finger on his nose for emphasis)* She went out and she bought you a house! *(The explosion comes from* WALTER *at the end of the revelation and he jumps up and turns away from all of them in a fury.* MAMA *continues, to* TRAVIS*)* You glad about the house? It's going to be yours when you get to be a man.

TRAVIS Yeah—I always wanted to live in a house.

MAMA All right, gimme some sugar then—*(*TRAVIS *puts his arms around her neck as she watches her son over the boy's shoulder. Then, to* TRAVIS, *after the embrace)* Now when you say your prayers tonight, you thank God and your grandfather—'cause it was him who give you the house—in his way.

RUTH *(Taking the boy from* MAMA *and pushing him toward the bedroom)* Now you get out of here and get ready for your beating.

TRAVIS Aw, Mama—

RUTH Get on in there—*(Closing the door behind him and turning radiantly to her mother-in-law)* So you went and did it!

MAMA *(Quietly, looking at her son with pain)* Yes, I did.

RUTH *(Raising both arms classically)* PRAISE GOD! *(Looks at* WALTER *a moment, who says nothing. She crosses rapidly to her husband)* Please, honey—let me be glad . . . you be glad too. *(She has laid her hands on his shoulders, but he shakes himself free of her roughly, without turning to face her)* Oh Walter . . .

a home . . . *a home. (She comes back to* MAMA*)* Well—
where is it? How big is it? How much it going to cost?

MAMA Well—

RUTH When we moving?

MAMA *(Smiling at her)* First of the month.

RUTH *(Throwing back her head with jubilance)* Praise
God!

MAMA *(Tentatively, still looking at her son's back turned
against her and* RUTH*)* It's—it's a nice house too . . . *(She
cannot help speaking directly to him. An imploring quality in her voice, her manner, makes her almost like a girl
now)* Three bedrooms—nice big one for you and
Ruth. . . . Me and Beneatha still have to share our room,
but Travis have one of his own—and *(With difficulty)* I
figure if the—new baby—is a boy, we could get one of
them double-decker outfits . . . And there's a yard with
a little patch of dirt where I could maybe get to grow
me a few flowers . . . And a nice big basement . . .

RUTH Walter honey, be glad—

MAMA *(Still to his back, fingering things on the table)*
'Course I don't want to make it sound fancier than it
is . . . It's just a plain little old house—but it's made good
and solid—and it will be *ours*. Walter Lee—it makes a
difference in a man when he can walk on floors that
belong to *him* . . .

RUTH Where is it?

MAMA *(Frightened at this telling)* Well—well—it's out
there in Clybourne Park—
  *(*RUTH'S *radiance fades abruptly, and* WALTER *finally
  turns slowly to face his mother with incredulity and
  hostility)*

RUTH Where?

MAMA *(Matter-of-factly)* Four o six Clybourne Street, Clybourne Park.

RUTH Clybourne Park? Mama, there ain't no colored people living in Clybourne Park.

MAMA *(Almost idiotically)* Well, I guess there's going to be some now.

WALTER *(Bitterly)* So that's the peace and comfort you went out and bought for us today!

MAMA *(Raising her eyes to meet his finally)* Son—I just tried to find the nicest place for the least amount of money for my family.

RUTH *(Trying to recover from the shock)* Well—well—'course I ain't one never been 'fraid of no crackers, mind you—but—well, wasn't there no other houses nowhere?

MAMA Them houses they put up for colored in them areas way out all seem to cost twice as much as other houses. I did the best I could.

RUTH *(Struck senseless with the news, in its various degrees of goodness and trouble, she sits a moment, her fists propping her chin in thought, and then she starts to rise, bringing her fists down with vigor, the radiance spreading from cheek to cheek again)* Well —well!—All I can say is—if this is my time in life— MY TIME—to say good-bye—*(And she builds with momentum as she starts to circle the room with an exuberant, almost tearfully happy release)*—to these goddamned cracking walls!—*(She pounds the walls)* —and these marching roaches!—*(She wipes at an imaginary army of marching roaches)*—and this cramped little closet which ain't now or never was no kitchen! ... then I say it loud and good, HALLELUJAH! AND

GOOD-BYE MISERY . . . I DON'T NEVER WANT TO SEE YOUR UGLY FACE AGAIN! *(She laughs joyously, having practically destroyed the apartment, and flings her arms up and lets them come down happily, slowly, reflectively, over her abdomen, aware for the first time perhaps that the life therein pulses with happiness and not despair)* Lena?

MAMA *(Moved, watching her happiness)* Yes, honey?

RUTH *(Looking off)* Is there—is there a whole lot of sunlight?

MAMA *(Understanding)* Yes, child, there's a whole lot of sunlight.
(Long pause)

RUTH *(Collecting herself and going to the door of the room* TRAVIS *is in)* Well—I guess I better see 'bout Travis. *(To* MAMA*)* Lord, I sure don't feel like whipping nobody today!
(She exits)

MAMA *(The mother and son are left alone now and the mother waits a long time, considering deeply, before she speaks)* Son—you—you understand what I done, don't you? *(*WALTER *is silent and sullen)* I—I just seen my family falling apart today . . . just falling to pieces in front of my eyes . . . We couldn't of gone on like we was today. We was going backwards 'stead of forwards—talking 'bout killing babies and wishing each other was dead . . . When it gets like that in life—you just got to do something different, push on out and do something bigger . . . *(She waits)* I wish you say something, son . . . I wish you'd say how deep inside you you think I done the right thing—

WALTER *(Crossing slowly to his bedroom door and finally turning there and speaking measuredly)* What you need me to say you done right for? *You* the head of this family. You run our lives like you want to. It was your money and you did what you wanted with it. So what you need for me to say it was all right for? *(Bitterly, to hurt her as deeply as he knows is possible)* So you butchered up a dream of mine—you—who always talking 'bout your children's dreams . . .

MAMA Walter Lee—

> *(He just closes the door behind him.* MAMA *sits alone, thinking heavily)*

Curtain

SCENE TWO

Time: Friday night. A few weeks later.
  *At rise: Packing crates mark the intention of the family
to move.* BENEATHA *and* GEORGE *come in, presumably from
an evening out again.*

GEORGE O.K. . . . O.K., whatever you say . . . *(They both
  sit on the couch. He tries to kiss her. She moves away)*
  Look, we've had a nice evening; let's not spoil it, huh? . . .
    *(He again turns her head and tries to nuzzle in and she
    turns away from him, not with distaste but with mo-
    mentary lack of interest; in a mood to pursue what
    they were talking about)*

BENEATHA I'm *trying* to talk to you.

GEORGE We always talk.

BENEATHA Yes—and I love to talk.

GEORGE *(Exasperated; rising)* I know it and I don't mind
  it sometimes . . . I want you to cut it out, see—The
  moody stuff, I mean. I don't like it. You're a nice-looking
  girl . . . all over. That's all you need, honey, forget the
  atmosphere. Guys aren't going to go for the atmosphere—they're going to go for what they see. Be glad
  for that. Drop the Garbo routine. It doesn't go with you.
  As for myself, I want a nice—*(Groping)*—simple
  (Thoughtfully)—sophisticated girl . . . not a poet—
  O.K.?
    *(He starts to kiss her, she rebuffs him again and he
    jumps up)*

BENEATHA Why are you angry, George?

GEORGE Because this is stupid! I don't go out with you
  to discuss the nature of "quiet desperation" or to hear

all about your thoughts—because the world will go on thinking what it thinks regardless—

BENEATHA Then why read books? Why go to school?

GEORGE *(With artificial patience, counting on his fingers)* It's simple. You read books—to learn facts—to get grades—to pass the course—to get a degree. That's all—it has nothing to do with thoughts.
(A long pause)

BENEATHA I see. *(He starts to sit)* Good night, George. *(GEORGE looks at her a little oddly, and starts to exit. He meets MAMA coming in)*

GEORGE Oh—hello, Mrs. Younger.

MAMA Hello, George, how you feeling?

GEORGE Fine—fine, how are you?

MAMA Oh, a little tired. You know them steps can get you after a day's work. You all have a nice time tonight?

GEORGE Yes—a fine time. A fine time.

MAMA Well, good night.

GEORGE Good night. *(He exits. MAMA closes the door behind her)* Hello, honey. What you sitting like that for?

BENEATHA I'm just sitting.

MAMA Didn't you have a nice time?

BENEATHA No.

MAMA No? What's the matter?

BENEATHA Mama, George is a fool—honest. *(She rises)*

MAMA *(Hustling around unloading the packages she has entered with. She stops)* Is he, baby?

BENEATHA Yes.
(BENEATHA *makes up* TRAVIS' *bed as she talks*)

MAMA You sure?

BENEATHA Yes.

MAMA Well—I guess you better not waste your time with
no fools.
(BENEATHA *looks up at her mother, watching her put
groceries in the refrigerator. Finally she gathers up her
things and starts into the bedroom. At the door she
stops and looks back at her mother*)

BENEATHA Mama—

MAMA Yes, baby—

BENEATHA Thank you.

MAMA For what?

BENEATHA For understanding me this time.
(*She exits quickly and the mother stands, smiling a
little, looking at the place where* BENEATHA *just stood.*
RUTH *enters*)

RUTH Now don't you fool with any of this stuff, Lena—

MAMA Oh, I just thought I'd sort a few things out. Is
Brother here?

RUTH Yes.

MAMA (*With concern*) Is he—

RUTH (*Reading her eyes*) Yes.
(MAMA *is silent and someone knocks on the door.*
MAMA *and* RUTH *exchange weary and knowing
glances and* RUTH *opens it to admit the neighbor,*
MRS. JOHNSON,* *who is a rather squeaky wide-*

---

*This character and the scene of her visit were cut from the original pro-
duction and early editions of the play.

*eyed lady of no particular age, with a newspaper under
her arm)*

MAMA *(Changing her expression to acute delight and a
ringing cheerful greeting)* Oh—hello there, Johnson.

JOHNSON *(This is a woman who decided long ago to be
enthusiastic about EVERYTHING in life and she is inclined to wave her wrist vigorously at the height of her
exclamatory comments)* Hello there, yourself! H'you
this evening, Ruth?

RUTH *(Not much of a deceptive type)* Fine, Mis' Johnson,
h'you?

JOHNSON Fine. *(Reaching out quickly, playfully, and pat-
ting RUTH'S stomach)* Ain't you starting to poke out none
yet! *(She mugs with delight at the overfamiliar remark
and her eyes dart around looking at the crates and packing preparation; MAMA'S face is a cold sheet of endur-
ance)* Oh, ain't we getting ready 'round here, though!
Yessir! Lookathere! I'm telling you the Youngers is really
getting ready to "move on up a little higher!"—Bless
God!

MAMA *(A little drily, doubting the total sincerity of the
Blesser)* Bless God.

JOHNSON He's good, ain't He?

MAMA Oh yes, He's good.

JOHNSON I mean sometimes He works in mysterious
ways . . . but He works, don't He!

MAMA *(The same)* Yes, he does.

JOHNSON I'm just sooooo happy for y'all. And this here
child—*(About RUTH)* looks like she could just pop open
with happiness, don't she. Where's all the rest of the
family?

MAMA Bennie's gone to bed—

JOHNSON Ain't no . . . *(The implication is pregnancy)* sickness done hit you—I hope . . . ?

MAMA No—she just tired. She was out this evening.

JOHNSON *(All is a coo, an emphatic coo)* Aw—ain't that lovely. She still going out with the little Murchison boy?

MAMA *(Drily)* Ummmm huh.

JOHNSON That's lovely. You sure got lovely children, Younger. Me and Isaiah talks all the time 'bout what fine children you was blessed with. We sure do.

MAMA Ruth, give Mis' Johnson a piece of sweet potato pie and some milk.

JOHNSON Oh honey, I can't stay hardly a minute—I just dropped in to see if there was anything I could do. *(Accepting the food easily)* I guess y'all seen the news what's all over the colored paper this week . . .

MAMA No—didn't get mine yet this week.

JOHNSON *(Lifting her head and blinking with the spirit of catastrophe)* You mean you ain't read 'bout them colored people that was bombed out their place out there?

(RUTH straightens with concern and takes the paper and reads it. JOHNSON notices her and feeds commentary)

JOHNSON Ain't it something how bad these here white folks is getting here in Chicago! Lord, getting so you think you right down in Mississippi! *(With a tremendous and rather insincere sense of melodrama)* 'Course I thinks it's wonderful how our folks keeps on pushing out. You hear some of these Negroes 'round here talking 'bout how they don't go where they ain't wanted and all that—but not me, honey! *(This is a lie)* Wilhemenia

Othella Johnson goes anywhere, any time she feels like it! *(With head movement for emphasis)* Yes I do! Why if we left it up to these here crackers, the poor niggers wouldn't have nothing—*(She clasps her hand over her mouth)* Oh, I always forgets you don't 'low that word in your house.

MAMA *(Quietly, looking at her)* No—I don't 'low it.

JOHNSON *(Vigorously again)* Me neither! I was just telling Isaiah yesterday when he come using it in front of me—I said, "Isaiah, it's just like Mis' Younger says all the time—"

MAMA Don't you want some more pie?

JOHNSON No—no thank you; this was lovely. I got to get on over home and have my midnight coffee. I hear some people say it don't let them sleep but I finds I can't close my eyes right lessen I done had that laaaast cup of coffee . . . *(She waits. A beat. Undaunted)* My Goodnight coffee, I calls it!

MAMA *(With much eye-rolling and communication between herself and* RUTH*)* Ruth, why don't you give Mis' Johnson some coffee.

   *(*RUTH *gives* MAMA *an unpleasant look for her kindness)*

JOHNSON *(Accepting the coffee)* Where's Brother tonight?

MAMA He's lying down.

JOHNSON Mmmmmm, he sure gets his beauty rest, don't he? Good-looking man. Sure is a good-looking man! *(Reaching out to pat* RUTH'S *stomach again)* I guess that's how come we keep on having babies around here. *(She winks at* MAMA*)* One thing 'bout Brother, he always know how to have a *good* time. And soooooo ambitious! I bet it was his idea y'all moving out to

Clybourne Park. Lord—I bet this time next month y'all's names will have been in the papers plenty—*(Holding up her hands to mark off each word of the headline she can see in front of her)* "NEGROES INVADE CLYBOURNE PARK—BOMBED!"

MAMA *(She and* RUTH *look at the woman in amazement)* We ain't exactly moving out there to get bombed.

JOHNSON Oh, honey—you know I'm praying to God every day that don't nothing like that happen! But you have to think of life like it is—and these here Chicago peckerwoods is some baaaad peckerwoods.

MAMA *(Wearily)* We done thought about all that Mis' Johnson.
(BENEATHA comes out of the bedroom in her robe and passes through to the bathroom. MRS. JOHNSON *turns)*

JOHNSON Hello there, Bennie!

BENEATHA *(Crisply)* Hello, Mrs. Johnson.

JOHNSON How is school?

BENEATHA *(Crisply)* Fine, thank you. *(She goes out.)*

JOHNSON *(Insulted)* Getting so she don't have much to say to nobody.

MAMA The child was on her way to the bathroom.

JOHNSON I know—but sometimes she act like ain't got time to pass the time of day with nobody ain't been to college. Oh—I ain't criticizing her none. It's just—you know how some of our young people gets when they get a little education. *(MAMA and* RUTH *say nothing, just look at her)* Yes—well. Well, I guess I better get on home. *(Unmoving)* 'Course I can understand how she must be proud and everything—being the only one in the family to make something of herself. I know just being a chauffeur ain't never satisfied Brother none. He shouldn't feel like that, though. Ain't nothing wrong with being a chauffeur.

MAMA There's plenty wrong with it.

JOHNSON What?

MAMA Plenty. My husband always said being any kind of a servant wasn't a fit thing for a man to have to be. He always said a man's hands was made to make things, or to turn the earth with—not to drive nobody's car for 'em—or—*(She looks at her own hands)* carry they slop jars. And my boy is just like him—he wasn't meant to wait on nobody.

JOHNSON *(Rising, somewhat offended)* Mmmmmmmmm. The Youngers is too much for me! *(She looks around)* You sure one proud-acting bunch of colored folks. Well—I always thinks like Booker T. Washington said that time—"Education has spoiled many a good plow hand"—

MAMA Is that what old Booker T. said?

JOHNSON He sure did.

MAMA Well, it sounds just like him. The fool.

JOHNSON *(Indignantly)* Well—he was one of our great men.

MAMA Who said so?

JOHNSON *(Nonplussed)* You know, me and you ain't never agreed about some things, Lena Younger. I guess I better be going—

RUTH *(Quickly)* Good night.

JOHNSON Good night. Oh—*(Thrusting it at her)* You can keep the paper! *(With a trill)* 'Night.

MAMA Good night, Mis' Johnson.
  (MRS. JOHNSON *exits*)

RUTH If ignorance was gold . . .

MAMA Shush. Don't talk about folks behind their backs.

RUTH You do.

MAMA I'm old and corrupted. (BENEATHA *enters*) You was
  rude to Mis' Johnson, Beneatha, and I don't like it at all.

BENEATHA (*At her door*) Mama, if there are two things
  we, as a people, have got to overcome, one is the Ku
  Klux Klan—and the other is Mrs. Johnson. (*She exits*)

MAMA Smart aleck.
  (*The phone rings*)

RUTH I'll get it.

MAMA Lord, ain't this a popular place tonight.

RUTH (*At the phone*) Hello—Just a minute. (*Goes to
  door*) Walter, it's Mrs. Arnold. (*Waits. Goes back to the
  phone. Tense*) Hello. Yes, this is his wife speaking . . . He's lying down now. Yes . . . well, he'll be in
  tomorrow. He's been very sick. Yes—I know we should
  have called, but we were so sure he'd be able to come in
  today. Yes—yes, I'm very sorry. Yes . . . Thank you very
  much. (*She hangs up.* WALTER *is standing in the doorway
  of the bedroom behind her*) That was Mrs. Arnold.

WALTER (*Indifferently*) Was it?

RUTH She said if you don't come in tomorrow that they
  are getting a new man . . .

WALTER Ain't that sad—ain't that crying sad.

RUTH She said Mr. Arnold has had to take a cab for three days . . . Walter, you ain't been to work for three days! *(This is a revelation to her)* Where you been, Walter Lee Younger? *(WALTER looks at her and starts to laugh)* You're going to lose your job.

WALTER That's right . . . *(He turns on the radio)*

RUTH Oh, Walter, and with your mother working like a dog every day—
    (A steamy, deep blues pours into the room)

WALTER That's sad too— Everything is sad.

MAMA What you been doing for these three days, son?

WALTER Mama—you don't know all the things a man what got leisure can find to do in this city . . . What's this—Friday night? Well—Wednesday I borrowed Willy Harris' car and I went for a drive . . . just me and myself and I drove and drove . . . Way out . . . way past South Chicago, and I parked the car and I sat and looked at the steel mills all day long. I just sat in the car and looked at them big black chimneys for hours. Then I drove back and I went to the Green Hat. *(Pause)* And Thursday—Thursday I borrowed the car again and I got in it and I pointed it the other way and I drove the other way—for hours—way, way up to Wisconsin, and I looked at the farms. I just drove and looked at the farms. Then I drove back and I went to the Green Hat. *(Pause)* And today—today I didn't get the car. Today I just walked. All over the Southside. And I looked at the Negroes and they looked at me and finally I just sat down on the curb at Thirty-ninth and South Parkway and I just sat there and watched the Negroes go by. And then I went to the Green Hat. You all sad? You all depressed? And you know where I am going right now—
    (RUTH goes out quietly)

MAMA Oh, Big Walter, is this the harvest of our days?

WALTER You know what I like about the Green Hat? I like this little cat they got there who blows a sax . . . He blows. He talks to me. He ain't but 'bout five feet tall and he's got a conked head and his eyes is always closed and he's all music—

MAMA *(Rising and getting some papers out of her handbag)* Walter—

WALTER And there's this other guy who plays the piano . . . and they got a sound. I mean they can work on some music . . . They got the best little combo in the world in the Green Hat . . . You can just sit there and drink and listen to them three men play and you realize that don't nothing matter worth a damn, but just being there—

MAMA I've helped do it to you, haven't I, son? Walter I been wrong.

WALTER Naw—you ain't never been wrong about nothing, Mama.

MAMA Listen to me, now. I say I been wrong, son. That I been doing to you what the rest of the world been doing to you. *(She turns off the radio)* Walter—*(She stops and he looks up slowly at her and she meets his eyes pleadingly)* What you ain't never understood is that I ain't got nothing, don't own nothing, ain't never really wanted nothing that wasn't for you. There ain't nothing as precious to me . . . There ain't nothing worth holding on to, money, dreams, nothing else—if it means—if it means it's going to destroy my boy. *(She takes an envelope out of her handbag and puts it in front of him and he watches her without speaking or moving)* I paid the man thirty-five hundred dollars down on the house. That leaves sixty-five hundred dollars. Monday morning

I want you to take this money and take three thousand dollars and put it in a savings account for Beneatha's medical schooling. The rest you put in a checking account—with your name on it. And from now on any penny that come out of it or that go in it is for you to look after. For you to decide. *(She drops her hands a little helplessly)* It ain't much, but it's all I got in the world and I'm putting it in your hands. I'm telling you to be the head of this family from now on like you supposed to be.

WALTER *(Stares at the money)* You trust me like that, Mama?

MAMA I ain't never stop trusting you. Like I ain't never stop loving you.
(She goes out, and WALTER sits looking at the money on the table. Finally, in a decisive gesture, he gets up, and, in mingled joy and desperation, picks up the money. At the same moment, TRAVIS enters for bed)

TRAVIS What's the matter, Daddy? You drunk?

WALTER *(Sweetly, more sweetly than we have ever known him)* No, Daddy ain't drunk. Daddy ain't going to never be drunk again. . . .

TRAVIS Well, good night, Daddy.
(The FATHER has come from behind the couch and leans over, embracing his son)

WALTER Son, I feel like talking to you tonight.

TRAVIS About what?

WALTER Oh, about a lot of things. About you and what kind of man you going to be when you grow up. . . . Son—son, what do you want to be when you grow up?

TRAVIS A bus driver.

WALTER *(Laughing a little)* A what? Man, that ain't nothing to want to be!

TRAVIS Why not?

WALTER 'Cause, man—it ain't big enough—you know what I mean.

TRAVIS I don't know then. I can't make up my mind. Sometimes Mama asks me that too. And sometimes when I tell her I just want to be like you—she says she don't want me to be like that and sometimes she says she does. . . .

WALTER *(Gathering him up in his arms)* You know what, Travis? In seven years you going to be seventeen years old. And things is going to be very different with us in seven years, Travis. . . . One day when you are seventeen I'll come home—home from my office downtown somewhere—

TRAVIS You don't work in no office, Daddy.

WALTER No—but after tonight. After what your daddy gonna do tonight, there's going to be offices—a whole lot of offices. . . .

TRAVIS What you gonna do tonight, Daddy?

WALTER You wouldn't understand yet, son, but your daddy's gonna make a transaction . . . a business transaction that's going to change our lives. . . . That's how come one day when you 'bout seventeen years old I'll come home and I'll be pretty tired, you know what I mean, after a day of conferences and secretaries getting things wrong the way they do . . . 'cause an executive's life is hell, man—*(The more he talks the farther away he gets)* And I'll pull the car up on the driveway . . . just a plain black Chrysler, I think, with white walls—no—black tires. More elegant. Rich people don't have to be flashy . . . though I'll have to get something a little sportier for Ruth—maybe a Cadillac convertible to do her shopping in. . . . And I'll come up the steps to the house and the gardener will be clipping away at the hedges and he'll say, "Good evening, Mr. Younger." And I'll say, "Hello, Jefferson, how are you this evening?" And I'll go inside and Ruth will come downstairs and meet me at the door and we'll kiss each other and she'll take my arm and we'll go up to your room to see you sitting on the floor with the catalogues of all the great schools in America around you. . . . All the great schools in the world! And—and I'll say, all right son—it's your seventeenth birthday, what is it you've decided? . . . Just tell me where you want to go to school and you'll *go*. Just tell me, what it is you want to be—and you'll *be* it. . . . Whatever you want to be—Yessir! *(He holds his arms open for* TRAVIS*)* You just name it, son . . . *(*TRAVIS *leaps into them)* and I hand you the world!

    *(*WALTER'S *voice has risen in pitch and hysterical promise and on the last line he lifts* TRAVIS *high)*

Blackout

SCENE THREE

Time: Saturday, moving day, one week later.

Before the curtain rises, RUTH'S *voice, a strident, dramatic church alto, cuts through the silence.*

It is, in the darkness, a triumphant surge, a penetrating statement of expectation: "Oh, Lord, I don't feel no ways tired! Children, oh, glory hallelujah!"

As the curtain rises we see that RUTH *is alone in the living room, finishing up the family's packing. It is moving day. She is nailing crates and tying cartons.* BENEATHA *enters, carrying a guitar case, and watches her exuberant sister-in-law.*

RUTH Hey!

BENEATHA *(Putting away the case)* Hi.

RUTH *(Pointing at a package)* Honey—look in that package there and see what I found on sale this morning at the South Center. *(*RUTH *gets up and moves to the package and draws out some curtains)* Lookahere—hand-turned hems!

BENEATHA How do you know the window size out there?

RUTH *(Who hadn't thought of that)* Oh—Well, they bound to fit something in the whole house. Anyhow, they was too good a bargain to pass up. *(*RUTH *slaps her head, suddenly remembering something)* Oh, Bennie—I meant to put a special note on that carton over there. That's your mama's good china and she wants 'em to be very careful with it.

BENEATHA I'll do it.
   *(*BENEATHA *finds a piece of paper and starts to draw large letters on it)*

RUTH You know what I'm going to do soon as I get in that new house?

BENEATHA What?

RUTH Honey—I'm going to run me a tub of water up to here . . . (*With her fingers practically up to her nostrils*) And I'm going to get in it—and I am going to sit . . . and sit . . . and sit in that hot water and the first person who knocks to tell me to hurry up and come out—

BENEATHA Gets shot at sunrise.

RUTH (*Laughing happily*) You said it, sister! (*Noticing how large* BENEATHA *is absent-mindedly making the note*) Honey, they ain't going to read that from no airplane.

BENEATHA (*Laughing herself*) I guess I always think things have more emphasis if they are big, somehow.

RUTH (*Looking up at her and smiling*) You and your brother seem to have that as a philosophy of life. Lord, that man—done changed so 'round here. You know—you know what we did last night? Me and Walter Lee?

BENEATHA What?

RUTH (*Smiling to herself*) We went to the movies. (*Looking at* BENEATHA *to see if she understands*) We went to the movies. You know the last time me and Walter went to the movies together?

BENEATHA No.

RUTH Me neither. That's how long it been. (*Smiling again*) But we went last night. The picture wasn't much good, but that didn't seem to matter. We went—and we held hands.

BENEATHA Oh, Lord!

RUTH We held hands—and you know what?

BENEATHA What?

RUTH When we come out of the show it was late and dark
and all the stores and things was closed up . . . and it
was kind of chilly and there wasn't many people on the
streets . . . and we was still holding hands, me and
Walter.

BENEATHA You're killing me.
(WALTER *enters with a large package. His happiness is deep in him; he cannot keep still with his
newfound exuberance. He is singing and wiggling
and snapping his fingers. He puts his package in
a corner and puts a phonograph record, which he
has brought in with him, on the record player. As
the music, soulful and sensuous, comes up he
dances over to* RUTH *and tries to get her to dance
with him. She gives in at last to his raunchiness and
in a fit of giggling allows herself to be drawn into
his mood. They dip and she melts into his arms in
a classic, body-melding "slow drag")*

BENEATHA (*Regarding them a long time as they dance,
then drawing in her breath for a deeply exaggerated comment which she does not particularly mean*) Talk
about—olddddddddddd-fashioneddddddd—Negroes!

WALTER (*Stopping momentarily*) What kind of Negroes?
(*He says this in fun. He is not angry with her
today, nor with anyone. He starts to dance with
his wife again*)

BENEATHA Old-fashioned.

WALTER (*As he dances with* RUTH) You know, when
these New Negroes have their convention—(*Pointing at
his sister*)—that is going to be the chairman of the

Committee on Unending Agitation. *(He goes on dancing, then stops)* Race, race, race! . . . Girl, I do believe you are the first person in the history of the entire human race to successfully brainwash yourself. *(BENEATHA breaks up and he goes on dancing. He stops again, enjoying his tease)* Damn, even the N double A C P takes a holiday sometimes! *(BENEATHA and RUTH laugh. He dances with RUTH some more and starts to laugh and stops and pantomimes someone over an operating table)* I can just see that chick someday looking down at some poor cat on an operating table and before she starts to slice him, she says . . . *(Pulling his sleeves back maliciously)* "By the way, what are your views on civil rights down there? . . ."

(He laughs at her again and starts to dance happily. The bell sounds)

BENEATHA Sticks and stones may break my bones but . . . words will never hurt me!

(BENEATHA goes to the door and opens it as WALTER and RUTH go on with the clowning. BENEATHA is somewhat surprised to see a quiet-looking middle-aged white man in a business suit holding his hat and a briefcase in his hand and consulting a small piece of paper)

MAN Uh—how do you do, miss. I am looking for a Mrs.— *(He looks at the slip of paper)* Mrs. Lena Younger? *(He stops short, struck dumb at the sight of the oblivious WALTER and RUTH)*

BENEATHA *(Smoothing her hair with slight embarrassment)* Oh—yes, that's my mother. Excuse me *(She closes the door and turns to quiet the other two)* Ruth! Brother! *(Enunciating precisely but soundlessly: "There's a white man at the door!" They stop dancing, RUTH cuts off the phonograph, BENEATHA opens the door. The man casts a curious quick glance at all of them)* Uh—come in please.

MAN *(Coming in)* Thank you.

BENEATHA My mother isn't here just now. Is it business?

MAN Yes . . . well, of a sort.

WALTER *(Freely, the Man of the House)* Have a seat. I'm Mrs. Younger's son. I look after most of her business matters.
   (RUTH and BENEATHA exchange amused glances)

MAN *(Regarding WALTER, and sitting)* Well—My name is Karl Lindner . . .

WALTER *(Stretching out his hand)* Walter Younger. This is my wife—*(RUTH nods politely)*—and my sister.

LINDNER How do you do.

WALTER *(Amiably, as he sits himself easily on a chair, leaning forward on his knees with interest and looking expectantly into the newcomer's face)* What can we do for you, Mr. Lindner!

LINDNER *(Some minor shuffling of the hat and briefcase on his knees)* Well—I am a representative of the Clybourne Park Improvement Association—

WALTER *(Pointing)* Why don't you sit your things on the floor?

LINDNER Oh—yes. Thank you. *(He slides the briefcase and hat under the chair)* And as I was saying—I am from the Clybourne Park Improvement Association and we have had it brought to our attention at the last meeting that you people—or at least your mother—has bought a piece of residential property at—*(He digs for the slip of paper again)*—four o six Clybourne Street . . .

WALTER That's right. Care for something to drink? Ruth, get Mr. Lindner a beer.

LINDNER *(Upset for some reason)* Oh—no, really. I mean thank you very much, but no thank you.

RUTH *(Innocently)* Some coffee?

LINDNER Thank you, nothing at all.
    (BENEATHA *is watching the man carefully*)

LINDNER Well, I don't know how much you folks know about our organization. *(He is a gentle man; thoughtful and somewhat labored in his manner)* It is one of these community organizations set up to look after—oh, you know, things like block upkeep and special projects and we also have what we call our New Neighbors Orientation Committee . . .

BENEATHA *(Drily)* Yes—and what do they do?

LINDNER *(Turning a little to her and then returning the main force to* WALTER*)* Well—it's what you might call a sort of welcoming committee, I guess. I mean they, we—I'm the chairman of the committee—go around and see the new people who move into the neighborhood and sort of give them the lowdown on the way we do things out in Clybourne Park.

BENEATHA *(With appreciation of the two meanings, which escape* RUTH *and* WALTER*)* Un-huh.

LINDNER And we also have the category of what the association calls—*(He looks elsewhere)*—uh—special community problems . . .

BENEATHA Yes—and what are some of those?

WALTER Girl, let the man talk.

LINDNER *(With understated relief)* Thank you. I would
sort of like to explain this thing in my own way. I mean
I want to explain to you in a certain way.

WALTER Go ahead.

LINDNER Yes. Well. I'm going to try to get right to the
point. I'm sure we'll all appreciate that in the long run.

BENEATHA Yes.

WALTER Be still now!

LINDNER Well—

RUTH *(Still innocently)* Would you like another chair—
you don't look comfortable.

LINDNER *(More frustrated than annoyed)* No, thank you
very much. Please. Well—to get right to the point I—*(A
great breath, and he is off at last)* I am sure you people
must be aware of some of the incidents which have happened in various parts of the city when colored people
have moved into certain areas—*(BENEATHA exhales
heavily and starts tossing a piece of fruit up and down
in the air)* Well—because we have what I think is going
to be a unique type of organization in American community life—not only do we deplore that kind of thing—
but we are trying to do something about it. *(BENEATHA
stops tossing and turns with a new and quizzical interest
to the man)* We feel—*(gaining confidence in his mission
because of the interest in the faces of the people he is
talking to)*—we feel that most of the trouble in this
world, when you come right down to it—*(He hits his
knee for emphasis)*—most of the trouble exists because
people just don't sit down and talk to each other.

RUTH *(Nodding as she might in church, pleased with the
remark)* You can say that again, mister.

LINDNER *(More encouraged by such affirmation)* That
we don't try hard enough in this world to understand
the other fellow's problem. The other guy's point of
view.

RUTH Now that's right.
   *(BENEATHA and WALTER merely watch and listen with
   genuine interest)*

LINDNER Yes—that's the way we feel out in Clybourne
Park. And that's why I was elected to come here this
afternoon and talk to you people. Friendly like, you
know, the way people should talk to each other and see
if we couldn't find some way to work this thing out. As
I say, the whole business is a matter of *caring* about the
other fellow. Anybody can see that you are a nice family
of folks, hard working and honest I'm sure. *(BENEATHA
frowns slightly, quizzically, her head tilted regarding
him)* Today everybody knows what it means to be on
the outside of *something*. And of course, there is always
somebody who is out to take advantage of people who
don't always understand.

WALTER What do you mean?

LINDNER Well—you see our community is made up of
people who've worked hard as the dickens for years
to build up that little community. They're not rich and
fancy people; just hard-working, honest people who
don't really have much but those little homes and a
dream of the kind of community they want to raise
their children in. Now, I don't say we are perfect and
there is a lot wrong in some of the things they want.
But you've got to admit that a man, right or wrong, has
the right to want to have the neighborhood he lives in
a certain kind of way. And at the moment the over-
whelming majority of our people out there feel that
people get along better, take more of a common interest

in the life of the community, when they share a common background. I want you to believe me when I tell you that race prejudice simply doesn't enter into it. It is a matter of the people of Clybourne Park believing, rightly or wrongly, as I say, that for the happiness of all concerned that our Negro families are happier when they live in their *own* communities.

BENEATHA *(With a grand and bitter gesture)* This, friends, is the Welcoming Committee!

WALTER *(Dumbfounded, looking at LINDNER)* Is this what you came marching all the way over here to tell us?

LINDNER Well, now we've been having a fine conversation. I hope you'll hear me all the way through.

WALTER *(Tightly)* Go ahead, man.

LINDNER You see—in the face of all the things I have said, we are prepared to make your family a very generous offer . . .

BENEATHA Thirty pieces and not a coin less!

WALTER Yeah?

LINDNER *(Putting on his glasses and drawing a form out of the briefcase)* Our association is prepared, through the collective effort of our people, to buy the house from you at a financial gain to your family.

RUTH Lord have mercy, ain't this the living gall!

WALTER All right, you through?

LINDNER Well, I want to give you the exact terms of the financial arrangement—

WALTER We don't want to hear no exact terms of no arrangements. I want to know if you got any more to tell us 'bout getting together?

LINDNER *(Taking off his glasses)* Well—I don't suppose that you feel . . .

WALTER Never mind how I feel—you got any more to say 'bout how people ought to sit down and talk to each other? . . . Get out of my house, man.
(He turns his back and walks to the door)

LINDNER *(Looking around at the hostile faces and reaching and assembling his hat and briefcase)* Well—I don't understand why you people are reacting this way. What do you think you are going to gain by moving into a neighborhood where you just aren't wanted and where some elements—well—people can get awful worked up when they feel that their whole way of life and everything they've ever worked for is threatened.

WALTER Get out.

LINDNER *(At the door, holding a small card)* Well—I'm sorry it went like this.

WALTER Get out.

LINDNER *(Almost sadly regarding* WALTER*)* You just can't force people to change their hearts, son.
(He turns and put his card on a table and exits. WALTER *pushes the door to with stinging hatred, and stands looking at it.* RUTH *just sits and* BENEATHA *just stands. They say nothing.* MAMA *and* TRAVIS *enter)*

MAMA Well—this all the packing got done since I left out of here this morning. I testify before God that my children got all the energy of the *dead*! What time the moving men due?

BENEATHA Four o'clock. You had a caller, Mama.
(She is smiling, teasingly)

MAMA Sure enough—who?

BENEATHA *(Her arms folded saucily)* The Welcoming Committee.
  (WALTER and RUTH giggle)

MAMA *(Innocently)* Who?

BENEATHA The Welcoming Committee. They said they're sure going to be glad to see you when you get there.

WALTER *(Devilishly)* Yeah, they said they can't hardly wait to see your face.
  (Laughter)

MAMA *(Sensing their facetiousness)* What's the matter with you all?

WALTER Ain't nothing the matter with us. We just telling you 'bout the gentleman who came to see you this afternoon. From the Clybourne Park Improvement Association.

MAMA What he want?

RUTH *(In the same mood as BENEATHA and WALTER)* To welcome you, honey.

WALTER He said they can't hardly wait. He said the one thing they don't have, that they just *dying* to have out there is a fine family of fine colored people! *(To RUTH and BENEATHA)* Ain't that right!

RUTH *(Mockingly)* Yeah! He left his card—

BENEATHA *(Handing card to MAMA)* In case.
  (MAMA reads and throws it on the floor—understanding and looking off as she draws her chair up to the table on which she has put her plant and some sticks and some cord)

MAMA Father, give us strength. *(Knowingly—and without fun)* Did he threaten us?

BENEATHA Oh—Mama—they don't do it like that any more. He talked Brotherhood. He said everybody ought to learn how to sit down and hate each other with good Christian fellowship.

(She and WALTER *shake hands to ridicule the remark)*

MAMA *(Sadly)* Lord, protect us . . .

RUTH You should hear the money those folks raised to buy the house from us. All we paid and then some.

BENEATHA What they think we going to do—eat 'em?

RUTH No, honey, marry 'em.

MAMA *(Shaking her head)* Lord, Lord, Lord . . .

RUTH Well—that's the way the crackers crumble. *(A beat)* Joke.

BENEATHA *(Laughingly noticing what her mother is doing)* Mama, what are you doing?

MAMA Fixing my plant so it won't get hurt none on the way . . .

BENEATHA Mama, you going to take *that* to the new house?

MAMA Un-huh—

BENEATHA That raggedy-looking old thing?

MAMA *(Stopping and looking at her)* It expresses ME!

RUTH *(With delight, to* BENEATHA*)* So there, Miss Thing! *(*WALTER *comes to* MAMA *suddenly and bends down behind her and squeezes her in his arms with all his strength. She is overwhelmed by the suddenness of it and, though delighted, her manner is like that of* RUTH *and* TRAVIS*)*

MAMA Look out now, boy! You make me mess up my thing here!

WALTER (*His face lit, he slips down on his knees beside her, his arms still about her*) Mama . . . you know what it means to climb up in the chariot?

MAMA (*Gruffly, very happy*) Get on away from me now . . .

RUTH (*Near the gift-wrapped package, trying to catch* WALTER'S *eye*) Psst—

WALTER What the old song say, Mama . . .

RUTH Walter—Now?
  (*She is pointing at the package*)

WALTER (*Speaking the lines, sweetly, playfully, in his mother's face*)
  I got wings . . . you got wings . . .
  All God's children got wings . . .

MAMA Boy—get out of my face and do some work . . .

WALTER
  When I get to heaven gonna put on my wings,
  Gonna fly all over God's heaven . . .

BENEATHA (*Teasingly, from across the room*) Everybody talking 'bout heaven ain't going there!

WALTER (*To* RUTH, *who is carrying the box across to them*) I don't know, you think we ought to give her that . . . Seems to me she ain't been very appreciative around here.

MAMA (*Eyeing the box, which is obviously a gift*) What is that?

WALTER (*Taking it from* RUTH *and putting it on the table in front of* MAMA) Well—what you all think? Should we give it to her?

RUTH Oh—she was pretty good today.

MAMA I'll good you—
(She turns her eyes to the box again)

BENEATHA Open it, Mama.
(She stands up, looks at it, turns and looks at all of them, and then presses her hands together and does not open the package)

WALTER *(Sweetly)* Open it, Mama. It's for you. *(MAMA looks in his eyes. It is the first present in her life without its being Christmas. Slowly she opens her package and lifts out, one by one, a brand-new sparkling set of gardening tools. WALTER continues, prodding)* Ruth made up the note—read it . . .

MAMA *(Picking up the card and adjusting her glasses)* "To our own Mrs. Miniver—Love from Brother, Ruth and Beneatha." Ain't that lovely . . .

TRAVIS *(Tugging at his father's sleeve)* Daddy, can I give her mine now?

WALTER All right, son. *(TRAVIS flies to get his gift)*

MAMA Now I don't have to use my knives and forks no more . . .

WALTER Travis didn't want to go in with the rest of us, Mama. He got his own. *(Somewhat amused)* We don't know what it is . . .

TRAVIS *(Racing back in the room with a large hatbox and putting it in front of his grandmother)* Here!

MAMA Lord have mercy, baby. You done gone and bought your grandmother a hat?

TRAVIS *(very proud)* Open it!
(She does and lifts out an elaborate, but very elaborate, wide gardening hat, and all the adults break up at the sight of it)

RUTH Travis, honey, what is that?

TRAVIS *(Who thinks it is beautiful and appropriate)* It's a gardening hat! Like the ladies always have on in the magazines when they work in their gardens.

BENEATHA *(Giggling fiercely)* Travis—we were trying to make Mama Mrs. Miniver—not Scarlett O'Hara!

MAMA *(Indignantly)* What's the matter with you all! This here is a beautiful hat! *(Absurdly)* I always wanted me one just like it!
(She pops it on her head to prove it to her grandson, and the hat is ludicrous and considerably oversized)

RUTH Hot dog! Go, Mama!

WALTER *(Doubled over with laughter)* I'm sorry, Mama—but you look like you ready to go out and chop you some cotton sure enough!
(They all laugh except MAMA, out of deference to TRAVIS' feelings)

MAMA *(Gathering the boy up to her)* Bless your heart— this is the prettiest hat I ever owned— *(WALTER, RUTH and BENEATHA chime in—noisily, festively and insincerely congratulating TRAVIS on his gift)* What are we all standing around here for? We ain't finished packin' yet. Bennie, you ain't packed one book.
(The bell rings)

BENEATHA That couldn't be the movers . . . it's not hardly two good yet—
(BENEATHA goes into her room. MAMA starts for door)

WALTER *(Turning, stiffening)* Wait—wait—I'll get it.
(He stands and looks at the door)

MAMA You expecting company, son?

WALTER *(Just looking at the door)* Yeah—yeah . . .
  (MAMA looks at RUTH, and they exchange innocent and unfrightened glances)

MAMA *(Not understanding)* Well, let them in, son.

BENEATHA *(From her room)* We need some more string.

MAMA Travis—you run to the hardware and get me some string cord.
  (MAMA goes out and WALTER turns and looks at RUTH. TRAVIS goes to a dish for money)

RUTH Why don't you answer the door, man?

WALTER *(Suddenly bounding across the floor to embrace her)* 'Cause sometimes it hard to let the future begin!
  (Stooping down in her face)
      I got wings! You got wings!
      All God's children got wings!
  (He crosses to the door and throws it open. Standing there is a very slight little man in a not too prosperous business suit and with haunted frightened eyes and a hat pulled down tightly, brim up, around his forehead. TRAVIS passes between the men and exits. WALTER leans deep in the man's face, still in his jubilance)
      When I get to heaven gonna put on my wings,
      Gonna fly all over God's heaven . . .
  (The little man just stares at him)
      Heaven—
  (Suddenly he stops and looks past the little man into the empty hallway) Where's Willy, man?

BOBO He ain't with me.

WALTER *(Not disturbed)* Oh—come on in. You know my wife.

BOBO *(Dumbly, taking off his hat)* Yes—h'you, Miss Ruth.

RUTH *(Quietly, a mood apart from her husband already, seeing BOBO)* Hello, Bobo.

WALTER You right on time today ... Right on time. That's the way! *(He slaps BOBO on his back)* Sit down ... lemme hear.
    (RUTH stands stiffly and quietly in back of them, as though somehow she senses death, her eyes fixed on her husband)

BOBO *(His frightened eyes on the floor, his hat in his hands)* Could I please get a drink of water, before I tell you about it, Walter Lee?
    (WALTER does not take his eyes off the man. RUTH goes blindly to the tap and gets a glass of water and brings it to BOBO)

WALTER There ain't nothing wrong, is there?

BOBO Lemme tell you—

WALTER Man—didn't nothing go wrong?

BOBO Lemme tell you—Walter Lee. *(Looking at RUTH and talking to her more than to WALTER)* You know how it was. I got to tell you how it was. I mean first I got to tell you how it was all the way ... I mean about the money I put in, Walter Lee ...

WALTER *(With taut agitation now)* What about the money you put in?

BOBO Well—it wasn't much as we told you—me and Willy—*(He stops)* I'm sorry, Walter. I got a bad feeling about it. I got a real bad feeling about it ...

WALTER Man, what you telling me about all this for? ... Tell me what happened in Springfield ...

BOBO Springfield.

RUTH *(Like a dead woman)* What was supposed to happen in Springfield?

BOBO *(To her)* This deal that me and Walter went into with Willy— Me and Willy was going to go down to Springfield and spread some money 'round so's we wouldn't have to wait so long for the liquor license . . . That's what we were going to do. Everybody said that was the way you had to do, you understand, Miss Ruth?

WALTER Man—what happened down there?

BOBO *(A pitiful man, near tears)* I'm trying to tell you, Walter.

WALTER *(Screaming at him suddenly)* THEN TELL ME, GODDAMMIT . . . WHAT'S THE MATTER WITH YOU?

BOBO Man . . . I didn't go to no Springfield, yesterday.

WALTER *(Halted, life hanging in the moment)* Why not?

BOBO *(The long way, the hard way to tell)* 'Cause I didn't have no reasons to . . .

WALTER Man, what are you talking about!

BOBO I'm talking about the fact that when I got to the train station yesterday morning—eight o'clock like we planned . . . Man—*Willy didn't never show up.*

WALTER Why . . . where was he . . . where is he?

BOBO That's what I'm trying to tell you . . . I don't know . . . I waited six hours . . . I called his house . . . and I waited . . . six hours . . . I waited in that train station six hours . . . *(Breaking into tears)* That was all the extra money I had in the world . . . *(Look-*

ing up at WALTER *with the tears running down his face*)
Man, *Willy is gone.*

WALTER Gone, what you mean Willy is gone? Gone
where? You mean he went by himself. You mean he
went off to Springfield by himself—to take care of getting the license—*(Turns and looks anxiously at* RUTH)
You mean maybe he didn't want too many people in
on the business down there? *(Looks to* RUTH *again, as
before)* You know Willy got his own ways. *(Looks
back to* BOBO) Maybe you was late yesterday and he
just went on down there without you. Maybe—maybe
—he's been callin' you at home tryin' to tell you what
happened or something. Maybe—maybe—he just got
sick. He's somewhere—he's got to be somewhere. We
just got to find him—me and you got to find him.
(Grabs BOBO *senselessly by the collar and starts to
shake him)* We got to!

BOBO *(In sudden angry, frightened agony)* What's the
matter with you, Walter! *When a cat take off with your
money he don't leave you no road maps!*

WALTER *(Turning madly, as though he is looking for
WILLY in the very room)* Willy!... Willy... don't
do it... Please don't do it... Man, not with that
money... Man, please, not with that money...
Oh, God... Don't let it be true... *(He is wandering around, crying out for* WILLY *and looking for him
or perhaps for help from God)* Man... I trusted you
... Man, I put my life in your hands... *(He starts
to crumple down on the floor as* RUTH *just covers her
face in horror.* MAMA *opens the door and comes into
the room, with* BENEATHA *behind her)* Man... *(He
starts to pound the floor with his fists, sobbing wildly)*
THAT MONEY IS MADE OUT OF MY FATHER'S
FLESH—

BOBO (*Standing over him helplessly*) I'm sorry, Walter
. . . (*Only* WALTER'S *sobs reply.* BOBO *puts on his hat*) I
had my life staked on this deal, too . . .
    (*He exits*)

MAMA (*To* WALTER) Son—(*She goes to him, bends down
to him, talks to his bent head*) Son . . . Is it gone? Son, I
gave you sixty-five hundred dollars. Is it gone? All of it?
Beneatha's money too?

WALTER (*Lifting his head slowly*) Mama . . . I never
. . . went to the bank at all . . .

MAMA (*Not wanting to believe him*) You mean . . .
your sister's school money . . . you used that too . . .
Walter? . . .

WALTER Yessss! All of it . . . It's all gone . . .
    (*There is total silence.* RUTH *stands with her face cov-
    ered with her hands;* BENEATHA *leans forlornly against
    a wall, fingering a piece of red ribbon from the mother's
    gift.* MAMA *stops and looks at her son without recog-
    nition and then, quite without thinking about it, starts
    to beat him senselessly in the face.* BENEATHA *goes to
    them and stops it*)

BENEATHA Mama!
    (MAMA *stops and looks at both of her children and
    rises slowly and wanders vaguely, aimlessly away from
    them*)

MAMA I seen . . . him . . . night after night . . . come in . . .
and look at that rug . . . and then look at me . . . the red
showing in his eyes . . . the veins moving in his head . . . I
seen him grow thin and old before he was
forty . . . working and working and working like somebody's old horse . . . killing himself . . . and you —you
give it all away in a day—(*She raises her arms to strike
him again*)

BENEATHA Mama—

MAMA Oh, God . . . *(She looks up to Him)* Look down here—and show me the strength.

BENEATHA Mama—

MAMA *(Folding over)* Strength . . .

BENEATHA *(Plaintively)* Mama . . .

MAMA Strength!

Curtain

ACT III

An hour later.

At curtain, there is a sullen light of gloom in the living room, gray light not unlike that which began the first scene of Act One. At left we can see WALTER *within his room, alone with himself. He is stretched out on the bed, his shirt out and open, his arms under his head. He does not smoke, he does not cry out, he merely lies there, looking up at the ceiling, much as if he were alone in the world.*

In the living room BENEATHA *sits at the table, still surrounded by the now almost ominous packing crates. She sits looking off. We feel that this is a mood struck perhaps an hour before, and it lingers now, full of the empty sound of profound disappointment. We see on a line from her brother's bedroom the sameness of their attitudes. Presently the bell rings and* BENEATHA *rises without ambition or interest in answering. It is* ASAGAI, *smiling broadly, striding into the room with energy and happy expectation and conversation.*

ASAGAI I came over . . . I had some free time. I thought I might help with the packing. Ah, I like the look of packing crates! A household in preparation for a journey! It depresses some people . . . but for me . . . it is another feeling. Something full of the flow of life, do you understand? Movement, progress . . . It makes me think of Africa.

BENEATHA Africa!

ASAGAI What kind of a mood is this? Have I told you how deeply you move me?

BENEATHA He gave away the money, Asagai . . .

ASAGAI Who gave away what money?

BENEATHA The insurance money. My brother gave it away.

ASAGAI Gave it away?

BENEATHA He made an investment! With a man even Travis wouldn't have trusted with his most worn-out marbles.

ASAGAI And it's gone?

BENEATHA Gone!

ASAGAI I'm very sorry . . . And you, now?

BENEATHA Me? . . . Me? . . . Me, I'm nothing . . . Me. When I was very small . . . we used to take our sleds out in the wintertime and the only hills we had were the ice-covered stone steps of some houses down the street. And we used to fill them in with snow and make them smooth and slide down them all day . . . and it was very dangerous, you know . . . far too steep . . . and sure enough one day a kid named Rufus came down too fast and hit the sidewalk and we saw his face just split open right there in front of us . . . And I remember standing there looking at his bloody open face thinking that was the end of Rufus. But the ambulance came and they took him to the hospital and they fixed the broken bones and they sewed it all up . . . and the next time I saw

Rufus he just had a little line down the middle of his face . . . I never got over that . . .

ASAGAI What?

BENEATHA That that was what one person could do for another, fix him up—sew up the problem, make him all right again. That was the most marvelous thing in the world . . . I wanted to do that. I always thought it was the one concrete thing in the world that a human being could do. Fix up the sick, you know—and make them whole again. This was truly being God . . .

ASAGAI You wanted to be God?

BENEATHA No—I wanted to cure. It used to be so important to me. I wanted to cure. It used to matter. I used to care. I mean about people and how their bodies hurt . . .

ASAGAI And you've stopped caring?

BENEATHA Yes—I think so.

ASAGAI Why?

BENEATHA *(Bitterly)* Because it doesn't seem deep enough, close enough to what ails mankind! It was a child's way of seeing things—or an idealist's.

ASAGAI Children see things very well sometimes—and idealists even better.

BENEATHA I know that's what you think. Because you are still where I left off. You with all your talk and dreams about Africa! You still think you can patch up the world. Cure the Great Sore of Colonialism—*(Loftily, mocking it)* with the Penicillin of Independence—!

ASAGAI Yes!

BENEATHA Independence *and then what?* What about all the crooks and thieves and just plain idiots who will come into power and steal and plunder the same as before—only now they will be black and do it in the name of the new Independence—WHAT ABOUT THEM?!

ASAGAI That will be the problem for another time. First we must get there.

BENEATHA And where does it end?

ASAGAI End? Who even spoke of an end? To life? To living?

BENEATHA An end to misery! To stupidity! Don't you see there isn't any real progress, Asagai, there is only one large circle that we march in, around and around, each of us with our own little picture in front of us—our own little mirage that we think is the future.

ASAGAI That is the mistake.

BENEATHA What?

ASAGAI What you just said about the circle. It isn't a circle—it is simply a long line—as in geometry, you know, one that reaches into infinity. And because we cannot see the end—we also cannot see how it changes. And it is very odd but those who see the changes—who dream, who will not give up—are called idealists . . . and those who see only the circle we call *them* the "realists"!

BENEATHA Asagai, while I was sleeping in that bed in there, people went out and took the future right out of my hands! And nobody asked me, nobody consulted me—they just went out and changed my life!

ASAGAI Was it your money?

BENEATHA What?

ASAGAI Was it your money he gave away?

BENEATHA It belonged to all of us.

ASAGAI But did you earn it? Would you have had it at all if your father had not died?

BENEATHA No.

ASAGAI Then isn't there something wrong in a house—in a world—where all dreams, good or bad, must depend on the death of a man? I never thought to see *you* like this, Alaiyo. You! Your brother made a mistake and you are grateful to him so that now you can give up the ailing human race on account of it! You talk about what good is struggle, what good is anything! Where are we all going and why are we bothering!

BENEATHA AND YOU CANNOT ANSWER IT!

ASAGAI *(Shouting over her)* I LIVE THE ANSWER! *(Pause)* In my village at home it is the exceptional man who can even read a newspaper . . . or who ever sees a book at all. I will go home and much of what I will have to say will seem strange to the people of my village. But I will teach and work and things will happen, slowly and swiftly. At times it will seem that nothing changes at all . . . and then again the sudden dramatic events which make history leap into the future. And then quiet again. Retrogression even. Guns, murder, revolution. And I even will have moments when I wonder if the quiet was not better than all that death and hatred. But I will look about my village at the illiteracy and disease and ignorance and I will not wonder long. And perhaps . . . perhaps I will be a great man . . . I mean perhaps I will hold on to the substance of truth and find my way always with the right course . . . and perhaps for it I will be butchered in my bed some night by the servants of empire . . .

BENEATHA *The martyr!*

ASAGAI (*He smiles*) ... or perhaps I shall live to be a very old man, respected and esteemed in my new nation ... And perhaps I shall hold office and this is what I'm trying to tell you, Alaiyo: Perhaps the things I believe now for my country will be wrong and outmoded, and I will not understand and do terrible things to have things my way or merely to keep my power. Don't you see that there will be young men and women—not British soldiers then, but my own black countrymen—to step out of the shadows some evening and slit my then useless throat? Don't you see they have always been there ... that they always will be. And that such a thing as my own death will be an advance? They who might kill me even ... actually replenish all that I was.

BENEATHA Oh, Asagai, I know all that.

ASAGAI Good! Then stop moaning and groaning and tell me what you plan to do.

BENEATHA Do?

ASAGAI I have a bit of a suggestion.

BENEATHA What?

ASAGAI (*Rather quietly for him*) That when it is all over— that you come home with me—

BENEATHA (*Staring at him and crossing away with exasperation*) Oh—Asagai—at this moment you decide to be romantic!

ASAGAI (*Quickly understanding the misunderstanding*) My dear, young creature of the New World—I do not mean across the city—I mean across the ocean: home—to Africa.

BENEATHA (*Slowly understanding and turning to him with murmured amazement*) To Africa?

ASAGAI Yes! . . . *(Smiling and lifting his arms playfully)*
Three hundred years later the African Prince rose up out
of the seas and swept the maiden back across the middle
passage over which her ancestors had come—

BENEATHA *(Unable to play)* To—to Nigeria?

ASAGAI Nigeria. Home. *(Coming to her with genuine romantic flippancy)* I will show you our mountains and our
stars; and give you cool drinks from gourds and teach
you the old songs and the ways of our people—and, in
time, we will pretend that—*(Very softly)*—you have only
been away for a day. Say that you'll come *(He swings
her around and takes her full in his arms in a kiss which
proceeds to passion)*

BENEATHA *(Pulling away suddenly)* You're getting me all
mixed up—

ASAGAI Why?

BENEATHA Too many things—too many things have happened today. I must sit down and think. I don't know
what I feel about anything right this minute.
*(She promptly sits down and props her chin on her
fist)*

ASAGAI *(Charmed)* All right, I shall leave you. No—don't
get up. *(Touching her, gently, sweetly)* Just sit awhile and
think . . . Never be afraid to sit awhile and think. *(He
goes to door and looks at her)* How often I have looked
at you and said, "Ah—so this is what the New World
hath finally wrought . . ."
*(He exits. BENEATHA sits on alone. Presently WALTER
enters from his room and starts to rummage through
things, feverishly looking for something. She looks up
and turns in her seat)*

BENEATHA *(Hissingly)* Yes—just look at what the New
World hath wrought! . . . Just look! *(She gestures with*

bitter disgust) There he is! *Monsieur le petit bourgeois noir*—himself! There he is—Symbol of a Rising Class! Entrepreneur! Titan of the system! *(WALTER ignores her completely and continues frantically and destructively looking for something and hurling things to floor and tearing things out of their place in his search. BENEATHA ignores the eccentricity of his actions and goes on with the monologue of insult)* Did you dream of yachts on Lake Michigan, Brother? Did you see yourself on that Great Day sitting down at the Conference Table, surrounded by all the mighty bald-headed men in America? All halted, waiting, breathless, waiting for your pronouncements on industry? Waiting for you— Chairman of the Board! *(WALTER finds what he is looking for—a small piece of white paper—and pushes it in his pocket and puts on his coat and rushes out without ever having looked at her. She shouts after him)* I look at you and I see the final triumph of stupidity in the world!

(The door slams and she returns to just sitting again. RUTH comes quickly out of MAMA'S room)

RUTH Who was that?

BENEATHA Your husband.

RUTH Where did he go?

BENEATHA Who knows—maybe he has an appointment at U.S. Steel.

RUTH *(Anxiously, with frightened eyes)* You didn't say nothing bad to him, did you?

BENEATHA Bad? Say anything bad to him? No—I told him he was a sweet boy and full of dreams and everything is strictly peachy keen, as the ofay kids say!

(MAMA enters from her bedroom. She is lost, vague, trying to catch hold, to make some sense of

*her former command of the world, but it still
eludes her. A sense of waste overwhelms her gait;
a measure of apology rides on her shoulders. She
goes to her plant, which has remained on the table,
looks at it, picks it up and takes it to the windowsill and sits it outside, and she stands and looks at
it a long moment. Then she closes the window, straightens her body with effort and turns around to her
children)*

MAMA Well—ain't it a mess in here, though? *(A false
cheerfulness, a beginning of something)* I guess we all
better stop moping around and get some work done. All
this unpacking and everything we got to do. *(RUTH raises
her head slowly in response to the sense of the line; and
BENEATHA in similar manner turns very slowly to look
at her mother)* One of you all better call the moving
people and tell 'em not to come.

RUTH Tell 'em not to come?

MAMA Of course, baby. Ain't no need in 'em coming all
the way here and having to go back. They charges for
that too. *(She sits down, fingers to her brow, thinking)*
Lord, ever since I was a little girl, I always remembers
people saying, "Lena—Lena Eggleston, you aims too
high all the time. You needs to slow down and see life
a little more like it is. Just slow down some." That's what
they always used to say down home—"Lord, that Lena
Eggleston is a high-minded thing. She'll get her due one
day!"

RUTH No, Lena . . .

MAMA Me and Big Walter just didn't never learn right.

RUTH Lena, no! We gotta go. Bennie—tell her . . .
*(She rises and crosses to BENEATHA with her arms out-
stretched. BENEATHA doesn't respond)* Tell her we

can still move . . . the notes ain't but a hundred and twenty-five a month. We got four grown people in this house—we can work . . .

MAMA *(To herself)* Just aimed too high all the time—

RUTH *(Turning and going to* MAMA *fast—the words pouring out with urgency and desperation)* Lena—I'll work . . . I'll work twenty hours a day in all the kitchens in Chicago . . . I'll strap my baby on my back if I have to and scrub all the floors in America and wash all the sheets in America if I have to—but we got to MOVE! We got to get OUT OF HERE!!

*(*MAMA *reaches out absently and pats* RUTH's *hand)*

MAMA No—I sees things differently now. Been thinking 'bout some of the things we could do to fix this place up some. I seen a secondhand bureau over on Maxwell Street just the other day that could fit right there. *(She points to where the new furniture might go.* RUTH *wanders away from her)* Would need some new handles on it and then a little varnish and it look like something brand-new. And—we can put up them new curtains in the kitchen . . . Why this place be looking fine. Cheer us all up so that we forget trouble ever come . . . *(To* RUTH*)* And you could get some nice screens to put up in your room 'round the baby's bassinet . . . *(She looks at both of them, pleadingly)* Sometimes you just got to know when to give up some things . . . and hold on to what you got. . . .

*(*WALTER *enters from the outside, looking spent and leaning against the door, his coat hanging from him)*

MAMA Where you been, son?

WALTER *(Breathing hard)* Made a call.

MAMA To who, son?

WALTER To The Man. *(He heads for his room)*

MAMA What man, baby?

WALTER *(Stops in the door)* The Man, Mama. Don't you know who The Man is?

RUTH Walter Lee?

WALTER *The Man.* Like the guys in the streets say—The Man. Captain Boss—Mistuh Charley . . . Old Cap'n Please Mr. Bossman . . .

BENEATHA *(Suddenly)* Lindner!

WALTER That's right! That's good. I told him to come right over.

BENEATHA *(Fiercely, understanding)* For what? What do you want to see him for!

WALTER *(Looking at his sister)* We going to do business with him.

MAMA What you talking 'bout, son?

WALTER Talking 'bout life, Mama. You all always telling me to see life like it is. Well—I laid in there on my back today . . . and I figured it out. Life just like it is. Who gets and who don't get. *(He sits down with his coat on and laughs)* Mama, you know it's all divided up. Life is. Sure enough. Between the takers and the "tooken." *(He laughs)* I've figured it out finally. *(He looks around at them)* Yeah. Some of us always getting "tooken." *(He laughs)* People like Willy Harris, they don't never get "tooken." And you know why the rest of us do? 'Cause we all mixed up. Mixed up bad. We get to looking 'round for the right and the wrong; and we worry about it and cry about it and stay up nights trying to figure out 'bout the wrong and the right of things all the time . . . And all the time, man, them takers is out there operating, just taking and taking. Willy Harris? Shoot—Willy Harris don't even count. He don't even count in the big scheme of things. But I'll say one thing for old Willy Harris . . . he's taught me something. He's taught me to keep my eye on what counts in this world. Yeah—*(Shouting out a little)* Thanks, Willy!

RUTH What did you call that man for, Walter Lee?

WALTER Called him to tell him to come on over to the show. Gonna put on a show for the man. Just what he wants to see. You see, Mama, the man came here today and he told us that them people out there where you want us to move—well they so upset they willing to pay us *not* to move! *(He laughs again)* And—and oh, Mama you would of been proud of the way me and Ruth and Bennie acted. We told him to get out . . . Lord have mercy! We told the man to get out! Oh, we was some proud folks this afternoon, yeah. *(He lights a cigarette)* We were still full of that old-time stuff . . .

RUTH *(Coming toward him slowly)* You talking 'bout taking them people's money to keep us from moving in that house?

WALTER I ain't just talking 'bout it, baby—I'm telling you that's what's going to happen!

BENEATHA Oh, God! Where is the bottom! Where is the real honest-to-God bottom so he can't go any farther!

WALTER See—that's the old stuff. You and that boy that was here today. You all want everybody to carry a flag and a spear and sing some marching songs, huh? You wanna spend your life looking into things and trying to find the right and the wrong part, huh? Yeah. You know what's going to happen to that boy someday

—he'll find himself sitting in a dungeon, locked in forever—and the takers will have the key! Forget it, baby! There ain't no causes—there ain't nothing but taking in this world, and he who takes most is smartest—and it don't make a damn bit of difference *how*.

MAMA You making something inside me cry, son. Some awful pain inside me.

WALTER Don't cry, Mama. Understand. That white man is going to walk in that door able to write checks for more money than we ever had. It's important to him and I'm going to help him . . . I'm going to put on the show, Mama.

MAMA Son—I come from five generations of people who was slaves and sharecroppers—but ain't nobody in my family never let nobody pay 'em no money that was a way of telling us we wasn't fit to walk the earth. We ain't never been that poor. (*Raising her eyes and looking at him*) We ain't never been that—dead inside.

BENEATHA Well—we are dead now. All the talk about dreams and sunlight that goes on in this house. It's all dead now.

WALTER What's the matter with you all! I didn't make this world! It was give to me this way! Hell, yes, I want me some yachts someday! Yes, I want to hang some real pearls 'round my wife's neck. Ain't she supposed to wear no pearls? Somebody tell me—tell me, who decides which women is suppose to wear pearls in this world. I tell you I am a *man*—and I think my wife should wear some pearls in this world!
(*This last line hangs a good while and* WALTER *begins to move about the room. The word "Man" has penetrated his consciousness; he mumbles it to himself repeatedly between strange agitated pauses as he moves about*)

MAMA Baby, how you going to feel on the inside?

WALTER Fine! . . . Going to feel fine . . . a man . . .

MAMA You won't have nothing left then, Walter Lee.

WALTER *(Coming to her)* I'm going to feel fine, Mama. I'm going to look that son-of-a-bitch in the eyes and say—*(He falters)*—and say, "All right, Mr. Lindner— *(He falters even more)*—that's *your* neighborhood out there! You got the right to keep it like you want! You got the right to have it like you want! Just write the check and—the house is yours." And—and I am going to say— *(His voice almost breaks)* "And you—you people just put the money in my hand and you won't have to live next to this bunch of stinking niggers! . . ." *(He straightens up and moves away from his mother, walking around the room)* And maybe—maybe I'll just get down on my black knees . . . *(He does so;* RUTH *and* BENNIE *and* MAMA *watch him in frozen horror)* "Captain, Mistuh, Bossman—*(Groveling and grinning and wringing his hands in profoundly anguished imitation of the slow-witted movie stereotype)* A-hee-hee-hee! Oh, yassuh boss! Yasssssuh! Great white—*(Voice breaking, he forces himself to go on)*—Father, just gi' ussen de money, fo' God's sake, and we's—we's ain't gwine come out deh and dirty up yo' white folks neighborhood . . ." *(He breaks down completely)* And I'll feel fine! Fine! FINE! *(He gets up and goes into the bedroom)*

BENEATHA That is not a man. That is nothing but a toothless rat.

MAMA Yes—death done come in this here house. *(She is nodding, slowly, reflectively)* Done come walking in my house on the lips of my children. You what supposed to be my beginning again. You—what supposed to be my harvest. *(To* BENEATHA*)* You—you mourning your brother?

BENEATHA He's no brother of mine.

MAMA What you say?

BENEATHA I said that that individual in that room is no brother of mine.

MAMA That's what I thought you said. You feeling like you better than he is today? *(BENEATHA does not answer)* Yes? What you tell him a minute ago? That he wasn't a man? Yes? You give him up for me? You done wrote his epitaph too—like the rest of the world? Well, who give you the privilege?

BENEATHA Be on my side for once! You saw what he just did, Mama! You saw him—down on his knees. Wasn't it you who taught me to despise any man who would do that? Do what he's going to do?

MAMA Yes—I taught you that. Me and your daddy. But I thought I taught you something else too . . . I thought I taught you to love him.

BENEATHA Love him? There is nothing left to love.

MAMA There is *always* something left to love. And if you ain't learned that, you ain't learned nothing. *(Looking at her)* Have you cried for that boy today? I don't mean for yourself and for the family 'cause we lost the money. I mean for him: what he been through and what it done to him. Child, when do you think is the time to love somebody the most? When they done good and made things easy for everybody? Well then, you ain't through learning—because that ain't the time at all. It's when he's at his lowest and can't believe in hisself 'cause the world done whipped him so! When you starts measuring somebody, measure him right, child, measure him right. Make sure you done taken into account what hills and valleys he come through before he got to wherever he is.

(TRAVIS bursts into the room at the end of the speech, leaving the door open)

TRAVIS Grandmama—the moving men are downstairs! The truck just pulled up.

MAMA *(Turning and looking at him)* Are they, baby? They downstairs?
(She sighs and sits. LINDNER appears in the doorway. He peers in and knocks lightly, to gain attention, and comes in. All turn to look at him)

LINDNER *(Hat and briefcase in hand)* Uh—hello . . .
(RUTH crosses mechanically to the bedroom door and opens it and lets it swing open freely and slowly as the lights come up on WALTER within, still in his coat, sitting at the far corner of the room. He looks up and out through the room to LINDNER)

RUTH He's here.
(A long minute passes and WALTER slowly gets up)

LINDNER *(Coming to the table with efficiency, putting his briefcase on the table and starting to unfold papers and unscrew fountain pens)* Well, I certainly was glad to hear from you people. *(WALTER has begun the trek out of the room, slowly and awkwardly, rather like a small boy, passing the back of his sleeve across his mouth from time to time)* Life can really be so much simpler than people let it be most of the time. Well—with whom do I negotiate? You, Mrs. Younger, or your son here? *(MAMA sits with her hands folded on her lap and her eyes closed as WALTER advances. TRAVIS goes closer to LINDNER and looks at the papers curiously)* Just some official papers, sonny.

RUTH Travis, you go downstairs—

MAMA *(Opening her eyes and looking into* WALTER'S*)* No. Travis, you stay right here. And you make him understand what you doing, Walter Lee. You teach him good. Like Willy Harris taught you. You show where our five generations done come to. *(*WALTER *looks from her to the boy, who grins at him innocently)* Go ahead, son—*(She folds her hands and closes her eyes)* Go ahead.

WALTER *(At last crosses to* LINDNER, *who is reviewing the contract)* Well, Mr. Lindner. *(*BENEATHA *turns away)* We called you—*(There is a profound, simple groping quality in his speech)*—because, well, me and my family *(He looks around and shifts from one foot to the other)* Well—we are very plain people . . .

LINDNER Yes—

WALTER I mean—I have worked as a chauffeur most of my life—and my wife here, she does domestic work in people's kitchens. So does my mother. I mean—we are plain people . . .

LINDNER Yes, Mr. Younger—

WALTER *(Really like a small boy, looking down at his shoes and then up at the man)* And—uh—well, my father, well, he was a laborer most of his life. . . .

LINDNER *(Absolutely confused)* Uh, yes—yes, I understand. *(He turns back to the contract)*

WALTER *(A beat; staring at him)* And my father—*(With sudden intensity)* My father almost *beat a man to death* once because this man called him a bad name or something, you know what I mean?

LINDNER *(Looking up, frozen)* No, no, I'm afraid I don't—

WALTER *(A beat. The tension hangs; then* WALTER *steps back from it)* Yeah. Well—what I mean is that we come from people who had a lot of *pride*. I mean—we are very proud people. And that's my sister over there and she's going to be a doctor—and we are very proud—

LINDNER Well—I am sure that is very nice, but—

WALTER What I am telling you is that we called you over here to tell you that we are very proud and that this— *(Signaling to* TRAVIS) Travis, come here. *(*TRAVIS *crosses and* WALTER *draws him before him facing the man)* This is my son, and he makes the sixth generation our family in this country. And we have all thought about your offer—

LINDNER Well, good . . . good—

WALTER And we have decided to move into our house because my father—my father—he earned it for us brick by brick. *(*MAMA *has her eyes closed and is rocking back and forth as though she were in church, with her head nodding the Amen yes)* We don't want to make no trouble for nobody or fight no causes, and we will try to be good neighbors. And that's *all* we got to say about that. *(He looks the man absolutely in the eyes)* We don't want your money. *(He turns and walks away)*

LINDNER *(Looking around at all of them)* I take it then— that you have decided to occupy . . .

BENEATHA That's what the man said.

LINDNER *(To* MAMA *in her reverie)* Then I would like to appeal to you, Mrs. Younger. You are older and wiser and understand things better I am sure . . .

MAMA I am afraid you don't understand. My son said we was going to move and there ain't nothing left for me to say. *(Briskly)* You know how these young folks is nowadays, mister. Can't do a thing with 'em! *(As he opens his mouth, she rises)* Good-bye.

LINDNER *(Folding up his materials)* Well—if you are that final about it . . . there is nothing left for me to say. *(He finishes, almost ignored by the family, who are concentrating on WALTER LEE. At the door LINDNER halts and looks around)* I sure hope you people know what you're getting into.
   (He shakes his head and exits)

RUTH *(Looking around and coming to life)* Well, for God's sake—if the moving men are here—LET'S GET THE HELL OUT OF HERE!

MAMA *(Into action)* Ain't it the truth! Look at all this here mess. Ruth, put Travis' good jacket on him . . . Walter Lee, fix your tie and tuck your shirt in, you look like somebody's hoodlum! Lord have mercy, where is my plant? *(She flies to get it amid the general bustling of the family, who are deliberately trying to ignore the nobility of the past moment)* You all start on down . . . Travis child, don't go empty-handed . . . Ruth, where did I put that box with my skillets in it? I want to be in charge of it myself . . . I'm going to make us the biggest dinner we ever ate tonight . . . Beneatha, what's the matter with them stockings? Pull them things up, girl . . .
   (The family starts to file out as two moving men appear and begin to carry out the heavier pieces of furniture, bumping into the family as they move about)

BENEATHA Mama, Asagai asked me to marry him today and go to Africa—

MAMA *(In the middle of her getting-ready activity)* He did? You ain't old enough to marry nobody—*(Seeing the moving men lifting one of her chairs precariously)*

Darling, that ain't no bale of cotton, please handle it so we can sit in it again! I had that chair twenty-five years . . .

(The movers sigh with exasperation and go on with their work)

BENEATHA *(Girlishly and unreasonably trying to pursue the conversation)* To go to Africa, Mama—be a doctor in Africa . . .

MAMA *(Distracted)* Yes, baby—

WALTER *Africa!* What he want you to go to Africa for?

BENEATHA To practice there . . .

WALTER Girl, if you don't get all them silly ideas out your head! You better marry yourself a man with some loot . . .

BENEATHA *(Angrily, precisely as in the first scene of the play)* What have you got to do with who I marry!

WALTER Plenty. Now I think George Murchison—

BENEATHA *George Murchison!* I wouldn't marry him if he was Adam and I was Eve!

(WALTER and BENEATHA go out yelling at each other vigorously and the anger is loud and real till their voices diminish. RUTH stands at the door and turns to MAMA and smiles knowingly)

MAMA *(Fixing her hat at last)* Yeah—they something all right, my children . . .

RUTH Yeah—they're something. Let's go, Lena.

MAMA *(Stalling, starting to look around at the house)* Yes—I'm coming. Ruth—

RUTH Yes?

MAMA *(Quietly, woman to woman)* He finally come into his manhood today, didn't he? Kind of like a rainbow after the rain . . .

RUTH *(Biting her lip lest her own pride explode in front of MAMA)* Yes, Lena.
(WALTER'S *voice calls for them raucously)*

WALTER *(Off stage)* Y'all come on! These people charges by the hour, you know!

MAMA *(Waving RUTH out vaguely)* All right, honey—go on down. I be down directly.
(RUTH hesitates, then exits. MAMA stands, at last alone in the living room, her plant on the table before her as the lights start to come down. She looks around at all the walls and ceilings and suddenly, despite herself, while the children call below, a great heaving thing rises in her and she puts her fist to her mouth to stifle it, takes a final desperate look, pulls her coat about her, pats her hat and goes out. The lights dim down. The door opens and she comes back in, grabs her plant, and goes out for the last time)

Curtain

ABOUT THE AUTHOR

LORRAINE HANSBERRY touched the taproots of American life as only a very few playwrights ever can in *A Raisin in the Sun,* the play that made her in 1959, at 29, the youngest American, the fifth woman, and the first black playwright to win the Best Play of the Year Award of the New York Drama Critics. In *Raisin,* wrote James Baldwin, "never before in the entire history of the American theater had so much of the truth of black people's lives been seen on the stage." Published and produced worldwide in over thirty languages and in thousands of productions nationally, the play "changed American theater forever" and became an American classic, as *The New York Times* summarized recently. In 1961, Hansberry's film adaptation of the play won a Cannes Festival Award and was nominated Best Screenplay; in the 1970s it was adapted into a Tony Award–winning musical; and in the 1980s a major resurgence began with revivals at a dozen regional theaters and the 1989 American Playhouse production for television of the complete play, unabridged for the first time.

On January 12, 1965, during the run of her second play, *The Sign in Sidney Brustein's Window,* cancer claimed Lorraine Hansberry. She was 34. "Her creative literary ability and her profound grasp of the deep social issues confronting the world today," predicted Martin Luther King, Jr., on her death, "will remain an inspiration to generations yet unborn." These words have proved prophetic as more and more of her work has become known.

To Be Young, Gifted and Black, a portrait of Hansberry in her own words, was the longest-running off-Broadway drama of 1969; it has been staged in every state of the Union, recorded, filmed, televised, and expanded into the widely read "informal autobiography" of the same title (not to be confused with the play), while the title itself (from her last speech) has entered the language. *Les Blancs* (The Whites), her drama of revolution in Africa, presented post-humously on Broadway, received the votes of six critics for Best American Play of 1970 and, since its acclaimed revival at the Arena Stage in 1988, has begun a resurgence of its own with productions planned at many regional theaters.

In her plays Hansberry illuminated the extraordinary lives and aspirations of "ordinary" people—black and white, American, African, and European—confronting the most fundamental challenges and choices of the century. Her published works include the above-mentioned plays, *To Be Young, Gifted and Black: An Informal Autobiography,* and *Lorraine Hansberry: The Collected Last Plays* and *The Movement,* a photohistory of the Civil Rights struggle. Excerpts from her speeches and interviews are recorded in the Caedmon album *Lorraine Hansberry Speaks Out: Art and the Black Revolution.*

LES BLANCS
The Collected Last Plays

"Hansberry, like the great Bernard Shaw, knew how to make
provocative characters become real people on the stage . . .
representing a variety of viewpoints on a subject of over-
whelming importance."
—*New York Daily News*

Les Blancs is a drama of Shakespearean grandeur set in the shift-
ing moral terrain of late-colonial Africa, where her anguished
hero must choose between two different kinds of loyalty and
two fatally opposing codes of conduct. *The Drinking Gourd*
traces the strangled interdependence of slaves, slave owners,
and overseers. And *What Use Are Flowers?* is a whimsical
yet deadly serious fantasy about the aftermath of a nuclear
conflagration.

"Somewhere, past performance, staging and written speech,
resides [the] brilliant anguished consciousness of Lorraine
Hansberry."
—*The New York Times*